THE

EVERYTHING®

ROBERT'S RULES BOOK

All you need to organize
and conduct a meeting

Barbara Campbell

Adams Media
Avon, Massachusetts

For Stephany

An Everything® Series Book.
Everything® and everything.com are registered trademarks of
F+W Publications, Inc.

Published by Adams Media, an F+W Publications Company
57 Littlefield Street, Avon, MA 02322 U.S.A.
www.adamsmedia.com

ISBN: 1-59337-124-1

Printed in Canada.

J I H G F E D C

Library of Congress Cataloging-in-Publication Data
Campbell, Barbara
The everything Robert's rules book / Barbara Campbell.
p.   cm.
(An everything series book)
ISBN 1-59337-124-1
1. Parliamentary practice. I. Robert, Henry M. (Henry Martyn), 1837-1923.
Robert's rules of order. II. Title. III. Series: Everything series.
JF515.C295 2004
060.4'2—dc22
2004002397

This publication is designed to provide accurate and authoritative information
with regard to the subject matter covered. It is sold with the understanding that
the publisher is not engaged in rendering legal, accounting, or other professional
advice. If legal advice or other expert assistance is required, the services of a
competent professional person should be sought.
    —From a *Declaration of Principles* jointly adopted by a Committee of the
American Bar Association and a Committee of Publishers and Associations

Many of the designations used by manufacturers and sellers to distinguish their
products are claimed as trademarks. Where those designations appear in this
book and Adams Media was aware of a trademark claim, the designations have
been printed with initial capital letters.

Cover illustrations by Barry Littmann.

This book is available at quantity discounts for bulk purchases.
For information, call 1-800-872-5627.

Welcome to the EVERYTHING® series!

THESE HANDY, accessible books give you all you need to tackle a difficult project, gain a new hobby, comprehend a fascinating topic, prepare for an exam, or even brush up on something you learned back in school but have since forgotten.

You can read an *EVERYTHING®* book from cover to cover or just pick out the information you want from our four useful boxes: e-facts, e-ssentials, e-alerts, and e-questions. We literally give you everything you need to know on the subject, but throw in a lot of fun stuff along the way, too.

We now have well over 300 *EVERYTHING®* books in print, spanning such wide-ranging topics as weddings, pregnancy, wine, learning guitar, one-pot cooking, managing people, and so much more. When you're done reading them all, you can finally say you know *EVERYTHING®*!

Ⓔ FACTS: Important sound bytes of information

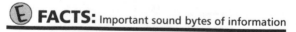

Ⓔ ESSENTIALS: Quick and handy tips

Ⓔ ALERTS!: Urgent warnings

Ⓔ QUESTIONS: Solutions to common problems

THE EVERYTHING® Series

Dear Reader,

Looking for an easy-to-understand, user-friendly way to make leading or participating in meetings, conferences, or seminars less challenging? *The Everything®
Robert's Rules Book* is just the book for you!

I've witnessed hundreds of meetings where Robert's Rules have been used, from governing bodies such as city councils and zoning boards to nonprofit organizations to social clubs and fraternal organizations to—well, you name it! Robert's Rules of Order have been used for more than a hundred years to provide a parliamentary procedure that is fair, orderly, and effective.

If you're looking over this book, chances are you'll be taking part in a meeting. *The Everything® Robert's
Rules Book* has been designed to introduce you to basic information you'll need to be an effective leader or participant. Real-life examples will be used and quick and easy tips offered to make this a stress-free introduction to Robert's Rules of Order, the most popular parliamentary procedure used not only in the United States but worldwide.

I hope you find the book informative and take it along to your next function for a convenient reference. And whatever your role there—whether it's as a participant or a leader—I wish you great success!

Sincerely,

Barbara Campbell

THE

EVERYTHING
Series

EDITORIAL

Publishing Director: Gary M. Krebs
Managing Editor: Kate McBride
Copy Chief: Laura MacLaughlin
Acquisitions Editor: Eric M. Hall
Development Editor: Karen Johnson Jacot
Production Editor: Jamie Wielgus

PRODUCTION

Production Director: Susan Beale
Production Manager: Michelle Roy Kelly
Series Designer: Daria Perreault
Cover Design: Paul Beatrice and Frank Rivera
Layout and Graphics: Colleen Cunningham,
Rachael Eiben, Michelle Roy Kelly,
John Paulhus, Daria Perreault, Erin Ring

Visit the entire Everything® series at everything.com

Acknowledgments

For my editors,
Eric M. Hall and Karen Johnson Jacot,
for their encouragement, support, and insight.

Contents

The Top Ten Reasons
to Learn Robert's Rules

1. Learning Robert's Rules is learning about how our country is run.

2. Robert's Rules are the leading authority on parliamentary procedure, not only in this country, but all around the world.

3. Meetings run smoother and are more orderly and productive when Robert's Rules are used.

4. The cornerstone of Robert's Rules is showing fairness to all. Democracy prevails when you use Robert's Rules in your meeting.

5. Robert's Rules are a minicourse in leadership.

6. You'll enjoy your group or organization more when you understand what's going on, and you'll want to participate more.

7. Protect your property rights—if you're a member of a homeowner's association, chances are you need to know Robert's Rules for its meetings.

8. A citizen who knows Robert's Rules can't be discounted; he knows how to make his voice heard.

9. Like a challenge? Want to exercise your mind, or develop the ability to better work with others? Learn Robert's Rules.

10. Robert's Rules are "the final word" on an issue—they are the authority that meeting leaders and group members consult. If that's what Robert's Rules say, that's that!

Introduction

TAPPED TO LEAD YOUR NEXT MEETING? Looking to speak up and make a difference at that next meeting, conference, or seminar? Don't want to lead but just want to do the best you can to put forward your point of view at your company, city commission, or school board meeting? *The Everything® Robert's Rules Book* is a modern, practical, easy-to-read guide that will take you step-by-step through the process.

If being a good communicator is vital to being a good leader, being a student of parliamentary procedure is vital to being a good participant at a meeting. Whether you're thrust into more leadership roles by your supervisors or you take on the challenge yourself for business or personal reasons, taking a little time to study the rules will help enormously to build your confidence and skill as a leader.

Robert's Rules are not only the most effective model for providing order at meetings, but they are the very essence of democracy in action—a model for the participation of the majority as well as the minority. Robert's Rules help define goals—who will be the designated leader and members of a group, what will be presented on an agenda, how old and new business will be discussed, and what entails a vote.

Organizations as diverse as governmental bodies to PTAs to motorcycle groups have used Robert's Rules. This book is an easy step-by-step guide to the most-used parliamentary procedures, and you will find it an invaluable resource whether you are a newcomer or simply want to know more. If you've ever picked up the latest edition of *Robert's Rules of Order,* you know it's a hefty read at 700-plus pages, with complex language and rules for situations that don't often occur. You might have been daunted at the prospect of finding the time and energy needed to study it.

Never before has saving time been more important for most people, whether it's in their professional or personal lives. Reading *The Everything® Robert's Rules Book* and applying what you learn will help you accomplish more in less time. This book is designed to help you grasp the concepts of parliamentary procedure as used in Robert's Rules in simple, easy-to-understand steps. Chapters are organized in a practical, straightforward pattern that has the particular procedure/concept outlined with the steps you'll need to use. A glossary of terms and terminology is at the rear of the book, with a list of places to consult for further study, such as helpful organizations and Web sites. In addition, a list of the most common motions is included for quick and easy reference.

Robert's Rules of Order have made many a good leader great, and have helped further our democratic ideals in this country by providing for an orderly forum for ideas. Congratulations on picking up the challenge of leadership!

Chapter 1
When People Meet

Studies have shown that people fear public speaking more than nuclear war. So it's no wonder you might be feeling a little apprehensive about speaking as a leader or a participant at a meeting—and being expected to know the rules of parliamentary procedure. Relax! This chapter will introduce you to the basics of proper meeting procedure so you will know what to expect and what to do to make your meeting run as smoothly and efficiently as possible.

Principles of Parliamentary Law

Simply put, the principles of parliamentary law are designed to provide for democracy in action. Meetings are run with fairness and in good faith. All members, not just the most vocal, are represented. All members have equal rights, privileges, and equal obligations.

In addition, each member has the right to understand the motions and discussions before the membership and know their effect: will fairness be shown to all? Will the rights of the majority *and* minority be protected? Parliamentary law provides a way for groups to arrive at the general will of their members in a reasonable time period and climate.

History

If you've ever lived in a planned development or a condominium, you know how important rules are to maintain order in a place where so many people live. Imagine, then, what it was like for the early colonists on the American continent who came from a structured government in Great Britain and found themselves in the wilderness without a plan for government.

Most people associate *Robert's Rules of Order* with the United States, but parliamentary law and procedure started with parliament in England around the thirteenth century. Some of the groups who traveled here by ship began to experiment with charters and other systems on the trip over, and before long, there were many strains of the parliamentary law hybrid sprouting up in the colonies.

The early settlers weren't just people in search of religious freedom. Some were businessmen and entrepreneurs, and some were politicians and military officers. It was natural for them to use the traditional parliamentary law developed in Great Britain in the thirteenth century, adapting it as needed. After all, they were proponents of change!

 FACT

> Governing boards, civic organizations, college fraternal groups—so many diverse groups have used Robert's Rules. Even groups that appear to have very diverse interests—such as civil rights groups and motorcycle enthusiast clubs—have successfully used the rules to conduct their meetings.

Thomas Jefferson and Parliamentary Practice

Most people know that Thomas Jefferson wrote the Declaration of Independence, but many don't know that he authored the *Manual of Parliamentary Practice*, published in 1801. There would be a need, after all, for a form of parliamentary law that would help those governing the new country. As "victims" of British oppression in the colonies, Jefferson and other American leaders wanted to make certain that the country had a working democratic government.

Jefferson drew up a plan for American government that used some elements of British parliamentary procedure, such as the rules for the British House of Commons. The U.S. Senate and the House of Representatives owe their procedure for running our government to Jefferson's plan.

A Good Idea Gets Duplicated

As the "big" governing organizations began doing their jobs, many other levels beneath them began to come into existence. Some of these were concerned with state and local governing bodies, but many weren't created to make or enforce laws. Other organizations from fraternal to business groups needed some form to guide their meeting business. After all, who wants to sound like the president of the United States at the local fraternal hall?

The Man Behind the Rules

Enter Henry Martyn Robert—a man who was apprehensive about being asked to lead a meeting. Not happy with the experience, Robert (1837–1923) decided to make a study of leading meetings. A West Point graduate who became a career U.S. Army officer, Robert spent time at various posts around the country. He became a student of parliamentary law, devouring Barclay's *Digest of Rules and Practices of the House*, and Cushing's *Manual of Parliamentary Practice: Rules of Proceeding and Debate in Deliberative Assemblies.* There were a number of other books on parliamentary procedure available at the time, but none that Robert was reported to have admired as much.

On-the-Job Training

Robert also devoted hours to attending meetings of various organizations in many different cities, where he realized that each group, each leader, and each membership ran the business of the organization differently. Perhaps it was his military experience that made him want to create order where there had been chaos. Everything that he read on the subject, every meeting that he attended, gave him the inspiration to create a book of rules for conducting meetings using parliamentary procedure.

And so was born *Robert's Rules of Order,* often imitated, but, as they say, never bettered.

Robert didn't find initial success—he had to publish his work on his own before he could interest a publisher. The book, with an initial print run of 4,000 copies, bore the title *Pocket Manual of Rules of Order for Deliberative Assemblies.* Whew! A new publisher changed the title to the much simpler *Robert's Rules of Order,* and the book has been in print ever since. Many organizations began using his form of parliamentary procedure to create uniformity where there had been so many different types of meetings run so many different ways.

Why Use Old Rules?

Although these rules were first published in the 1870s and are over 130 years old, they are not antiquated. Instead, they have stood the test of time and are considered as strong as ever. You don't have to endure the hundreds of hours of meeting attendance and parliamentary study that Robert did. Instead, learn from his experience!

 ESSENTIAL

Think about finding a mentor for your new role as a chair or presenter at meetings. Many people became successful by following the example of another successful person. Perhaps you can find a coworker, a supervisor, a friend, or someone prominent in your community who would mentor you.

Types of Meetings

Take a minute and think about the meeting you'll be leading or speaking at. What type of meeting is it? A business meeting? Civic group meeting? Fraternal organization meeting? Knowing will help you decide just how formal or informal your conduct and the conduct of the members should be, what its membership will be, the order of business, and so on.

Robert's Rules can be used at the most formal of meetings, and the most informal. The idea is to use the rules to encourage democratic debate (and corresponding code of conduct), to have a structure, and to have a roadmap for a desired outcome.

Here's a quick list of the basic types of meetings (more on each in Chapter 3):

- Regular meeting
- Special or called meeting
- Annual meeting
- Session
- Executive session
- Convention
- Adjourned meeting

More and more meetings are being conducted by means that were not in existence at the time that Robert wrote his book. Conducting meetings by audio conference (telephone conference call) or videoconference (televised conference) have become more efficient, less expensive ways to get groups together for meetings, especially when travel can be time-consuming and unpredictable these days. Meetings can also be conducted by e-mail and electronic chat room setups. There are pros and cons to each of these types of meetings that will be discussed further in Chapter 3.

You can use Robert's Rules as a guide to running any meeting of any type, whatever the setting. Take the time to make a study of them and you'll be assured of the most effective meetings you've led or attended. They are the leadership tool no one should be without in this fast-paced world.

 ALERT!

> There are a number of versions of *Robert's Rules of Order*. To prevent confusion, your group should decide which will be the official version to refer to if a question on procedure should arise.

Serving as the Chair

The results of a recent national study showed that the most important quality employers look for in a prospective employee is being a good communicator. They want someone who can be effective in both oral and written communication. In written communications like letters or e-mails, you can always take your time and reread, rewrite, and edit them before sending. But you don't have that advantage most of the time when you're speaking. People who are good at public speaking project first and foremost a confidence in what they're saying, and that's something you can learn only by doing it.

Since you're looking at leading a meeting or conference of some sort and you're researching *Robert's Rules of Order,* the first thing on your mind is how you're going to learn the structure of your job. One effective business technique is "look at the forest, not the trees." You can't possibly learn all of the rules in a short period—or even an extended period—of time. And it's likely you won't ever encounter some of the situations covered by the rules.

You know the goal you're after: to effectively run the meeting or conference. You know the outcome you want: to be successful. You know you have that distinctive something that made you the one others want to do the job (and yes, sometimes it's because they don't want to do it!). And finally, you are the type to want to rise to the challenge, to learn new things and be successful at them.

Presiding over a Meeting

If you're presiding, there are a number of things that you will do very quickly, very early on, that will establish the way you want to run the meeting and achieve the order that you desire for your group.

Set the Tone

No one wants a tyrant for a chair. Act like one once and you'll probably be ushered out of presiding very, very quickly. It's important to distinguish firm, authoritative behavior from dictatorship. Entering the room in a confident manner, dressing appropriately, and being prepared will go a long way toward establishing you as an effective leader. The respect you earn by these behaviors and the way you conduct the meeting will eliminate many problems and problem behaviors from people.

Call to Order

As a chair, you should call the meeting to order on time. It's expected that you will be on time, and you should then show your group that you do not wait for latecomers and waste the time of those who have been considerate and have arrived at the expected hour. Doing everything possible to save time without rushing things or appearing dictatorial or nitpicky will also help. Have agendas printed and ready to distribute. Seat those giving reports in the front of the room instead of scattered throughout the group so that the group doesn't have to wait for them to come forward. Be prepared to act or speak in a way that demonstrates courtesy, while insisting, if necessary, that order be maintained and that the participation and contributions of those attending be treated in a businesslike manner.

Speaking Out

Maybe you don't want to lead a meeting but you want to speak out for or against an issue or make your views known about an important topic. For instance, you feel passionate about fighting the expansion of the nearby airport or highway that will destroy the value and use of your home. Or you find out that your children's school desperately needs improvement or that a dangerous ex-convict has moved into your neighborhood. You're not interested in running a corporate meeting or becoming a whiz at the local legislative hearings.

If you're feeling that passionate about anything

similar to the above and you've picked up this book, it's obvious that you already know what you're going to need to do: be prepared to be an effective speaker, with relevant facts and opinions. You know how you must conduct yourself to have them heard at the meeting or hearing you attend. A quick, easy, basic understanding of this book will help guide you toward the challenge you've accepted—to make a difference.

 ESSENTIAL

> No time to attend outside meetings to learn more? Many local, state, and federal government meetings are televised, particularly on public television stations. Record them and watch them when it's convenient for you to do so.

Presenting Your View

If you've ever been reluctant to speak up at a meeting, particularly a meeting conducted with Robert's Rules, you may be feeling anxious about your performance. Don't be insecure! Your input is a valuable part of a deliberative assembly—a group that wants to think about, discuss intelligently, and vote responsibly on important issues!

What Do You Have to Present?

If you've picked up this book because you want to present your viewpoint at a meeting, you've given thought not only to what you have to say on an issue, but on how you will say it. This is very important in getting your message across. There are a few basic steps you should take to be successful.

- Dress appropriately. Don't let your clothes distract from your message.
- Adopt a calm demeanor when addressing the membership. It's admirable to be passionate about your issue, but stay calm and focused to convey your message effectively.
- Don't waste time. Be ready for your turn on the floor.
- Make eye contact as you speak. Don't read long passages from your notes, however brilliantly you've written what you want to say. If you feel the need, jot a few notes on note cards.
- Do not argue if confronted by a member who disagrees with you. After all, it's a deliberative assembly, where courtesy and the viewpoints of others are to be respected. Calmly restate your point and then, if you do not get your hoped-for action, gracefully accept a temporary defeat and think about regrouping and reintroducing the issue at a future meeting.

How Will You Present It?

There are two ways that you can speak on your issue at your meeting. Achieving the floor is the first step. This is done two different ways: make a motion or present a report as a member of a committee. See Chapter 6 for information on how to make a motion.

If you're presenting a report, consult with your board on what the format of it should be. The degree of formality will dictate the format of your report; some groups, especially work-related ones, require a very particular format.

 ALERT!

> One successful presenter admits to forgetting his own name when he nervously rose to speak for the first time at a meeting. To eliminate that possibility from ever occurring again, he wrote his name on his notes, just in case, so that he could surreptitiously glance at it!

Stand and Be Recognized

If the meeting is formal, you'll stand and wait until the chair recognizes you before making a motion. If the group is informal in nature, raise your hand. Always, in either setting, state your name unless the chair states it first. This is necessary to demonstrate courtesy to those who don't know you and for the formality of the secretary's noting your name in the minutes (the formal record of the meeting).

Ensuring You'll Speak

A group will consider more seriously the views of a member who has invested himself by taking on some responsibility for the group. This includes accepting appointments to committees and other tasks, which will demonstrate that you take the group seriously and want to help further its aims and improve it. Attend meetings regularly: A member who doesn't just attend when he wants to speak, but is there to promote the regular interests of the group, merits consideration.

Confronting Your Anxiety

Henry Martyn Robert is a terrific role model for those with anxiety over public speaking or implementing the rules. Thrust into leading a meeting and not happy about the job he did, he found a way to improve by observing meetings and reading up on the subject of running them. One of the most effective practices of a successful person (in her professional *and* personal life) is to imitate successful behavior and actions on the part of those she admires. It's why your mother wanted you to hang out with the "good" kids, after all! Study how others handle speaker anxiety.

Take a Cue

Successful speakers deal with anxiety. They don't just "get over it" after the first time. Most people will tell you they still have mild to moderate, sometimes even severe, anxiety before they speak at a meeting. But they know how to deal with it. They take a few moments alone to take some deep breaths, to calm themselves, to focus. Follow their example.

In the same way, many people who are urged to

lead or speak at meetings using Robert's Rules have anxiety over following the rules. They are concerned that they will not know what to do, that they'll make a mistake, and that they'll look foolish. Funny thing is, it'll probably happen sometime, even after you've become experienced with the rules. It just happens. Distractions at the meeting, a temporary lapse in attention, or just simple forgetfulness will probably (surely!) happen. But if you stay relaxed and stop trying to be perfect, you'll be fine!

 FACT

> Some people carry their fear of public speaking into leading or speaking at a meeting. If you're one of those people, don't let fear get the better of you! Face it down by taking a speech class, watching others speak, and even having a friend coach you. Soon that fear will be a thing of the past!

Anybody Have a Question?

In group situations, it is common for people to find it hard to ask a question. Perhaps it's human nature to want to look like we know everything even when we don't. Call it ego, or call it self-protection. But research has shown that wherever people gather, behind every person with a question are at least five more people who want to ask it but are afraid to do so. Be courageous!

If there's something you don't understand about Robert's Rules, ask a fellow member, especially someone you consider to be well informed about them. Remember, ignorance *isn't* bliss. Who wants to find out later that if you'd asked that question, you could have avoided a lot of problems?

Here's hoping you're feeling less anxious about leading a meeting or presenting at one. You'll find that the more you approach the task as something you can do to contribute and to build your skills, the better you'll do. You're likely to enjoy your group or organization more, too, when you lead or present than if you just attend, sit, and don't say much, then later complain about the way things are going. So push yourself a little, give this book a good read-through, and then keep it handy to give yourself confidence. You're already on the road to success if you've read this far!

Chapter 2
Keeping It Official

Officers are elected by the membership to serve the group or organization. Officers serve as role models for members and represent the best the group has to offer. Whether yours is a service group, a homeowner's association, a campus fraternal organization, or a social club, officers are the heart and hands of the membership. You'll also need to understand the hows and whys of creating bylaws (or rules) to govern your organization.

Running Deliberative Assemblies

Robert's Rules are concerned with the conduct of business in deliberative assemblies. What exactly is that? you might be wondering. Simply put, deliberative assemblies are groups that meet to conduct business—to consider all manner of ideas and proposals that can advance the purpose of the group.

A group of elected or appointed individuals that administers or manages a group may be considered to be a board. This board does not have a preset number of members decided by Robert's Rules, although it's usually smaller than the group it oversees. It may or may not function autonomously, that is, as an independent and self-governing body.

 FACT

> Edmund Burke is given credit for first using the term *deliberative assembly* when he discussed the English parliament in the late 1700s. He defined the term as "a group of persons meeting to make group decisions, to discuss and to determine a common course of action."

A board could be a number of people who make laws or govern a corporation. For instance, if it's part of a fraternal group or a club, the board probably administers the organization. Another example is the board of a Parent-Teacher Association (PTA). This board determines what matters will be addressed at a meeting, and oversees the spending of the group's money.

These and other similar boards do several things to make order the number-one priority so that business may be conducted. They decide on what authority will be used to establish the rules by which the group will be run. Many groups make Robert's Rules the authority on all issues pertaining to order and the way the group will be governed.

Who Are Your Officers?

Every group or organization needs at least two officers: a presiding officer and a secretary or clerk. Most groups need more. Larger groups, especially those that do service in the community, may have more officers and committees than other, smaller groups do.

Customary Offices

Most groups will have a chair or president, a vice president, a secretary, and a treasurer. Larger groups may also have a corresponding secretary. Depending on the size and purpose of your organization, you may also have directors, trustees, or managers who sit on an executive board; a historian; a librarian; a curator; a chaplain; a sergeant-at-arms; a doorkeeper; honorary officers; or even a parliamentarian. Some groups, particularly those that are governing bodies, even have an attorney.

Officer Qualifications, Please?

The duties and responsibilities of officers may differ widely among other groups and organizations. Particular groups have particular needs for officers—everything from specific experience and knowledge to personality traits—to make them run efficiently.

After all, who wants a president who has the personality of a tyrant, however qualified she is for the presidency? Especially if it's a club where people come to have a good time! Likewise, a group that is dedicated to community service may need someone savvy with grant writing to accomplish its goals.

 ESSENTIAL

> Officers have the same rights as members do to make motions, debate those motions, and vote. The only exception is the president, who is required to be impartial, and therefore has restricted rights in the group.

Do your bylaws state that there are qualifications for officers? Many do. There may be requirements that a candidate be a member for a certain length of time before becoming an officer. Some groups that handle large amounts of money require that prospective treasurers be subject to a criminal background check and be bonded.

The Officers' Roles

The jobs that officers perform should be clearly detailed in the bylaws of your group. Job descriptions should be very specific to the roles these officers will play in your group—don't try to save time by simply copying wording from another group (unless, perhaps, that group is very similar to yours). There are some generalities, however, that apply to the officers of most organizations.

The President

The office of president is the most important to a group or organization. The president doesn't just preside over the group; he leads by always using democratic principles in all areas of group business. A good president knows that election to the office doesn't mean the membership has handed over control to him exclusively.

 ALERT!

The president is the guardian of the rights of the members. She must make certain that members aren't subjected to motions whose purpose is to delay business or force one faction's wishes on all. The president also protects the membership from those who would disturb its democratic process in any way during meetings.

Presiding over the Group

In some organizations, the president helps set and carry out the goals, while in others her primary duty is to preside over meetings and elections. As president, she acts and speaks for the group, supervises any employees, and signs legal documents, all according to the bylaws.

 QUESTION?

Is that the royal "we"?
The presiding officer should always refer to herself in the third person when talking to the membership. For example, the chair should say, "The chair rules that . . . " Others address the president as Mr. or Ms. President.

The president usually serves as the chair of the meeting or appoints another to perform this job. The president should be very familiar with the bylaws, rules of the group, and parliamentary procedure, especially the particular version of Robert's Rules the group uses. She must be knowledgeable and impartial in running meetings and all activities, and should be able to work well with other officers, including the secretary, with whom she will prepare meeting agendas.

Staying Impartial

As the presiding officer, the president loses certain rights that other members enjoy. The president can't make motions or engage in debate without stepping down and turning over the duties of running the meeting. He must not resume chairing the meeting until the motion has been disposed of by a vote or other action.

The president can vote only if his vote breaks a tie vote, if it would create a tie vote (and that's what's desired by the president), or if it's a ballot vote. (To truly stay impartial, a ballot vote is always best. See Chapter 13 for more on voting.) Additionally, the president must always step down from presiding over any motion in which he has a personal or financial interest.

The Vice President

Being a vice president is good training for being a high-wire walker. She has an interest in becoming president, or there would be no point in being vice president since it's a precursor to that higher office. On the other hand, there can never be any indication of eagerness to assume that office until the president's term is up.

 ESSENTIAL

The organization's bylaws should detail how the vice president assumes the office of president if the office is vacated before the end of a term. Does the vice president automatically become the president? Must there be another election? Look to your bylaws for the final word.

Of course, the vice president takes over for the president if he has to leave office early for any reason. The vice president also presides over meetings at the president's request or if disciplinary action is being taken against the president. When the vice president presides, he or she should be addressed as Mr. or Ms. President.

The Secretary

Groups and organizations must have at least two officers to conduct a meeting: the president and the secretary. The president presides, but the secretary has a great deal of important work to do as well. The duties that many group secretaries perform include (but aren't limited to): helping prepare agendas, keeping all the records of the group and maintaining an accurate list of the membership, notifying members of regular and special meetings, taking the minutes and signing certain documents required by the bylaws, maintaining all official documents of the group (such as bylaws), and bringing bylaws and any necessary supplies (such as agendas, ballots, etc.) to meetings.

The Treasurer

The treasurer's main responsibility is to take charge of the organization's money. He receives dues and writes receipts for the members, deposits the group's money in the bank, balances and reconciles the checking account, and pays bills as authorized by the membership and/or bylaws.

Obviously, there may be less money for the treasurer to deal with and fewer bills to pay in smaller groups; larger groups may have more money and larger bills to pay. Some groups may also have employees, in which case the treasurer is responsible for writing paychecks and deducting such things as Social Security taxes and income taxes. The treasurer is responsible for preparing a budget, submitting it to the group for approval, and keeping financial records for annual audits. Group bylaws and standing rules spell out other duties.

 ALERT!

> The group treasurer should *never* deposit group money into his personal checking account. Additionally, any group that handles a large amount of money should have the treasurer bonded.

Parliamentary Inquiry

The president of a group or organization is expected to know more about running a meeting than the average member does. As the person who chairs most meetings, he is the person to whom members will address parliamentary inquiries. Is it in order to move that the question being considered be postponed to next month's meeting? a member might ask, or, could the chair clarify a motion the member doesn't understand? At what time will a certain matter be brought up at tonight's meeting that was postponed from last month's meeting?

Sometimes a parliamentary inquiry is made by a member to alert the membership that a potential problem exists. Is a member making a motion to close debate? Do the other members realize what this means—how it will affect the rights of those who have not had the opportunity to speak for or against a motion?

 ESSENTIAL

> To make a parliamentary inquiry, all a member has to do is state, "I rise to a parliamentary inquiry." The chair should respond by asking the member to state her inquiry. Then the member will ask the question.

Sometimes things aren't the way they should be. The chair isn't bringing forward old business or bringing up new business or doesn't notice that parliamentary procedure isn't being followed. A point of order could be raised in some cases, but a more diplomatic, more subtle way of doing things sometimes is to make a parliamentary inquiry. It's a way of stopping matters for a moment and asking the question in such a way that the chair may realize what's happening and correct it.

Officer Reports

Having officers in charge of business and having them give reports is a lot like having committees studying a matter—both save groups or organizations time and effort. There's an additional benefit as well: Officers are elected and members of committees appointed on the basis of an individual's skills and experience. A group treasurer is often a member who is experienced with handling money matters; a group secretary is often a professional person accustomed to keeping accurate business records. The officers bring expertise to the table to benefit the entire group.

Officers present reports on specific matters relating to their office, tasks they have been given, and responsibilities outlined by your group's bylaws. These reports are scheduled to be given at meetings (both orally and in writing) at a frequency level determined by the bylaws, or by the matter itself being reported on. If, for instance, your group is constructing a new clubhouse, reports may be requested on a frequent basis.

The Secretary Reports

The secretary is in charge of taking minutes. This record of what transpires at each meeting is so important that for most groups and organizations, going over the minutes from the last meeting will be the first priority after the meeting is called to order. Time can be saved in approving the minutes by using general consent to get majority approval; if a member feels there is an inaccuracy, he should call it to the attention of the chair. Any inaccuracies can then be corrected and approved.

If a mistake in the minutes is noticed later, a member must use the motion to amend something previously adopted (see Chapter 9). Corrections are noted in the margins of the minutes. The date of acceptance and the secretary's initials should be included there as well.

 ESSENTIAL

> There is no statute of limitations on corrections of the minutes. They may be corrected even years later, as long as there is a two-thirds vote, a majority vote with previous notice, a majority vote of the entire membership, or unanimous consent.

Show Me the Money!

New treasurers should always be given (or should request) copies of past reports in order to duplicate the format. The treasurer's report for small groups is simple: just a listing of the balance on hand at the beginning of the month being discussed, total receipts (income), total disbursements, and the balance on hand at the end of the month. If the group desires, income and disbursements can be detailed (listing the source and the amount of the income), and the specifics of the expenditures (such as postage, printing, and so on) can be listed.

For a large group, the same format is used, but a more detailed report will likely be required when there are large amounts of money involved. Also, the treasurer may be paying employees and accompanying taxes; treasurers for large groups are often experienced in bookkeeping, accounting, and income tax payments, and so on. Treasurers should always sign their reports.

An audit should be conducted on the treasurer's books to make certain that they are being kept correctly and that they are accurate. In small groups, the audit may be done by a committee; in larger groups that handle a lot of money and expenditures, it's better to bring in an outside auditor.

Other Reports

Reports may also be generated by committees and boards. The report itself should be kept as brief as possible without leaving out important information. The officer or committee members sign the reports before they are presented to the membership. A summary of these reports should be included in the minutes, and copies of the full reports should be attached and kept in the minutes binder.

 ALERT!

Reports are only as good as the care given them. Mistakes, even simple spelling errors, reflect badly on the professionalism of the officer or committee. Proofread, spellcheck, even have someone else look over your report so that it is a good reflection on you and your office.

Keeping the Minutes

The secretary takes notes of what business is conducted at meetings. These are the minutes, the official written record that will be kept as long as the group or organization directs. What is included in the minutes? Everything that happened—but not in *minute* detail! Remember that the minutes are read at the next meeting, and no one wants a blow-by-blow account that lasts as long as the meeting did.

The agenda is the guideline to what will be addressed at a meeting, so the secretary should keep it at hand for easy reference. A useful tool for the secretary is a copy of the agenda that has extra space between each agenda item for notes. New secretaries should always study the minutes of past meetings to see how they're done.

The minutes themselves should include the reports of officers and committees, and special orders or elections of officers. Any unfinished business is also included, and the secretary should make note of this for himself for agenda-making time so he's sure to include it for the next meeting. New business is documented. This should include what motions were made, what action was taken on them, and who made them. The person who seconded the motion doesn't have to be mentioned unless it is the policy of your group to do so.

If there was a program presented, there should be mention of it in the minutes, as well as any announcements that were made. Election results are very important, as are points of order and the chair's rulings on them. The hour of adjournment should be noted. The secretary should type and sign the minutes and initial any changes that are jotted in the margin at the next meeting. As always, the minutes should be proofread and spellchecked for accuracy.

ESSENTIAL

Some groups tape-record their meetings. This way, the secretary or others can refer back to the tapes for the sake of accuracy. Sometimes people speak too quickly for even the most efficient note takers; other times there may be a member who challenges what the secretary noted. Having a tape recording available will help settle disputes quickly.

Creating Bylaws

Your group's bylaws are the foundation of your group or organization, the rules by which it will govern itself. A group without bylaws will almost certainly dissolve into chaos. Weak bylaws create a weak organization; well-thought-out, well-planned bylaws equal a strong organization.

Who Writes Them

Bylaws are usually best made by a bylaws committee comprising a mixture of types of individuals—

those with common sense, some foresight, and a strong sense of democratic principles. Does your group have the type of individuals in it that can be of service in creating bylaws? Do they have the knowledge and experience with parliamentary procedure to write the rules that will run the organization? Some people truly love setting up the structure of a group or organization. You've just got to find those people.

The bylaws committee may need the advice of a parliamentarian. The names and Web addresses of organizations that may be of help in this area are listed in Appendix C. If your organization is large or there will be financial and legal issues, you may need the advice of a qualified attorney to review your bylaws.

What's Included

Bylaws must be detailed enough to give a group an "operating manual" but not so focused on minutiae that they look as if they were drawn up by a committee of nitpickers. They should be drawn up at the time of the formation of the group, but they can always be changed at the mandate of the membership, with proper notice and either a two-thirds or majority vote—depending on what is written in the bylaws!

It's important that you specify in your bylaws which particular edition of Robert's Rules the organization will use as the governing manual for parliamentary procedure; remember, don't just insert a phrase that states that "Robert's Rules will be used." This makes it too hard later when something is challenged to determine which book you're referring to. Be very specific: *"The Everything® Robert's Rules Book,* Adams Media, 2004, will be used."

Checklist for Bylaws

There's no one-size-fits-all set of bylaws, and for a very good reason. Imagine trying to make a set of bylaws that would encompass all the varieties of groups and organizations that exist. The bylaws would be either so specific that they would fill hundreds of pages and take a law background to understand, or they would be so ambiguous you would feel like you were treading on quicksand every time you looked for a particular rule.

The following list will help guide your group as it writes or amends its bylaws.

- **The organization's name.** Article I should state the organization's name. Make certain that it's written the same way throughout your bylaws.
- **Object or purpose (mission statement).** Article II should state, in a sentence or two, the mission statement; that is, the object of or purpose for the group.
- **Members.** Article III should detail what types of members your group will include: active, inactive, honorary, and so on. What rights will the members have? What limitations will be imposed on each type? How do people apply for membership? What

makes them eligible? (If the group is open to the public, it is important not to discriminate.) Will you detail requirements such as attending a certain number of meetings? What's to be done with a member who disrupts meetings or otherwise behaves in a manner unbecoming to a member of your group? If a member wants to resign, what is the procedure for doing so?

- **Officers.** Article IV should detail the officers, their ranking, and their duties, as well as state how they are nominated and elected. Will all members be eligible to serve as officers? What is the term of office? How will vacancies, should they occur, be filled? What are the grounds for removing an officer? (Filling a vacancy and removing an officer are much the same, so these actions should require a two-thirds vote.)

- **Meetings.** Article V specifies the day and time for meetings, what quorum is required for meetings, what business can be taken care of, and the procedure for calling special meetings.

- **Executive board.** Article VI should discuss the executive board of your group. What's the composition of the board? When will it have meetings? What's the policy for removal from office and filling vacancies? What are the executive board's duties? How much power do you want to give to the board? Shall it decide matters like spending or borrowing money, signing contracts, or other serious actions without the vote of the membership? If the group is large and has employees, is the board in charge of employee matters?

- **Committees.** Article VII should state what committees the group will have, such as social, membership, finance, and so on, and the duties of committee members. Who appoints the committees? Can they spend money?

- **Parliamentary authority.** Article VIII should state the book that will be the bible to be consulted regarding questions of parliamentary procedure.

- **Amendments.** Article IX covers amending the bylaws. It should state how these bylaws (which have been so carefully thought out and written up) may be changed (certainly not quickly or easily, or without previous notice and a two-thirds vote!).

 QUESTION?

Who gets the most power?
Consider the balance of power when you are creating bylaws. Do you want your officers or your membership to hold most of the power in the group? A balance is probably best for your group.

These are not the only areas or topics that need to be in your group's bylaws. However, the list serves as a good guideline. If there is a group or organization similar to yours, the bylaws committee might consider asking it to borrow a copy of its bylaws for consultation purposes.

Keep the bylaws as clear and concise as you can. Legalese is definitely not in order; avoid making the language sound like attorneys wrote it and only other attorneys can understand it (unless yours is a governing body of some kind). Remember that bylaws are meant to be a framework of rules that govern your group but do not become unnecessarily restrictive.

Chapter 3
Now in Session

There are many different types of meetings, sessions, and assemblies of organizations. Knowing the differences can help you and your group decide what type will best suit your needs, and where and how often it should be held. Some organizations need to meet often, some need few meetings. Does your organization have a big annual meeting? Does it even need to? This chapter covers the organizational know-how you'll need to get your group's business done.

Defining the Terms

Some of the terms for gatherings of people to conduct business have become blurred by their use—and misuse—over the years. To prevent confusion, some definitions may be helpful. When your group writes or revises its bylaws, specifying exactly what each means can prevent misinterpretation in the future. The bylaws should also state who provides notice of a meeting, who may call a special meeting or session, and so on.

Is It a Meeting?

Meetings are official gatherings of members to take care of business for a time period; traditionally this time period might have a recess, but no break longer than that. Guests may be present along with the members but they are not permitted to take part in the business part of the meeting. Sometimes there is a social part to the meeting, but most of the time, a meeting is held for the purpose of conducting the business of the group or organization.

An organization may have regularly scheduled meetings, as well as occasionally calling a special meeting, which may be necessary due to an emergency or some complex matter requiring more time than a regular meeting. The scheduling process of both regular and special meetings should be specified in the organization's bylaws. Sometimes members find it easier to remember meetings that are scheduled to take place on "the first Monday of the month" or with similar regularity.

Some groups or organizations may hold an annual meeting at which elections may be held; officers, boards, and standing committees may present reports; and so on. Occasionally these bigger meetings may be held biannually or by some schedule that suits the group or organization. Again, bylaws should state when, where, and how often all types of meetings should be held and what notice is required to hold them.

Is It a Session?

A session is defined as a series of meetings to conduct a single order of business. This might be a conference or convention that takes place over several days. Sometimes the U.S. Congress and state legislatures meet in a special session to conduct a single type of business such as budgetary issues. If a group finds it can't take care of all its business at one meeting, it could choose to adjourn and hold another meeting a day or a week later to finish the business, if this is allowed in the bylaws.

Executive Sessions

The term *executive meeting* or *session* can be confusing—generally, it is any part of a meeting (or an entire meeting) in which the proceedings are to be secret. Guests are not allowed into such meetings, for obvious reasons. The board of officers might meet in executive session to discuss issues that require private discussion. Again, look at your bylaws to determine if an executive session may be held, who it may be called by, and how notice must be given.

 ESSENTIAL

> The membership at a session can't enact business that interferes with any other future session. They should also not postpone a motion past the time of the session as a way to prevent others from addressing the issue of the motion.

Conventions

Many large groups or organizations have a convention at which they conduct business each year or every other year and which often includes educational programs. At this meeting, officers are often elected and annual or biannual reports are read. Sometimes official papers or positions are announced. If there are matters to be voted upon, it's important to have a credentials committee to oversee who can or can't vote. The bylaws should contain language specifying the purpose, conduct, and role of a convention.

Are We Adjourned?

The term *adjourned meeting* can be confusing, because many people think once a meeting is adjourned it is concluded. But an adjourned meeting indicates a continuation—a regular or special meeting that will be held at a later time but before the next regular session. This meeting is to help finish business that can't be taken care of in one meeting.

The term *meeting is adjourned* means that the meeting is concluded, that it is not to be continued. This is said at the end of a regular meeting. A member may make a motion to adjourn or the chair can adjourn a meeting by general consent (which is explained later in this chapter).

Where Shall We Meet?

The place in which a group or organization meets is very important to its effectiveness. How many members are there? Is the place convenient to the majority of members? Is it conducive to the meeting—with comfortable seating, effective lighting, audiovisual equipment if necessary—and a place where members and guests will feel welcome?

Obviously you will have difficulty having an effective meeting in a place that is physically uncomfortable or where the sound quality is so bad that members will have trouble hearing or participating and feel alienated. Officers and members may need a place to make notes during the meeting or write on a blackboard or put visual material on a standing easel.

Say, Wouldn't It Be Easier To . . . ?

Technology in the form of computers, e-mails, faxes, videoconferencing, and so on has improved so dramatically that many people have wondered if one day we won't need to meet at all. Wouldn't it be easier, for instance, to have a meeting by e-mail? they wonder. Robert's Rules emphasize the importance of the participation of members in free and open discussion of an issue. This requires the presence of members all at one time for such a discussion (and vote).

Imagine the difficulty of getting everyone together at one time for an online meeting. Then imagine how difficult it would be to wade through the dozens of instantaneous requests to speak, to object, and so on! Interruptions in electrical power and Internet access can also occur. The list of potential problems could go on and on and on. There could be innumerable challenges to a group's actions if meetings were conducted by e-mail at this point in the development of technology. (Not to mention that there are still people who do not have computers or Internet access.)

Then Let's Put Everyone on TV!

Videoconferencing has been a good tool for businesses for some time, and some groups and organizations are trying it for regular meetings. This technology enables a meeting to take place when members are at different locations. While the spirit of Robert's Rules in regard to the immediate and open participation of members is more evident here than in the e-mail suggestion, many parliamentarians still object to this type of meeting because it can restrain the immediacy of participants' responses.

FACT

Audio (telephone) conferences are an alternative to meetings, but they can be problematic: It's easy for there to be simultaneous talking, which makes it difficult for the chair to keep order. Videoconferencing remains more popular with more groups and organizations because of the ability to see the participants.

How Often Shall We Meet?

It can be hard for a group of people to decide how often to meet. Too often, and you have members who say they have other things to do. Too seldom, and there's likely to be too much business to transact. If you have difficulty getting a quorum (the legal number of members who must be present to conduct business), then it can be an even longer meeting when everyone is finally gathered together.

These days, most people will agree that they have too many meetings, and that meetings are taking too long. Talk to members of similar organizations about how often they meet and what works best for them. Generally, many fraternal organizations and nonprofit organizations find that meeting once a month suits their needs. If there is a significant problem getting a quorum during summer months, or during months containing holidays, then an alternate schedule can be arranged and meetings can be postponed during those months. It can't be stated enough that language about meeting times, dates, and so on needs to be in the group's bylaws.

 ESSENTIAL

> A recess is a short break in a meeting lasting anywhere from a few minutes to a few hours. It's best to call for one in a long meeting so that people have a chance to stretch their legs or get something to eat if it's a daylong meeting.

Creating a Meeting Environment

Meetings will be much more effective if you've done everything to make them comfortable and conducive to your goals. Robert's Rules are flexible on meeting places—whatever is best for your group or organization, is the rule of thumb. Observing the arrangement of meeting space that other groups have used can be helpful. If you're having a small meeting, placing seats in a semicircle can lend a more informal air and promote a sense that all members are treated alike. For more formal meetings, it may be necessary to have the chair and the group's officers seated in front of the members.

Look Who Just Came In

Keep distractions to a minimum. If the meeting is in a banquet meeting room, for instance, try to keep the members from being seated so that they can see into the kitchen (watching food being prepared may be distracting!). Have the entrance and exit from the room at the rear of the membership, not where the comings and goings of others will take focus from the meeting.

Inviting and Excusing Guests

Perhaps you are planning an agenda that involves a special program that includes guests. But you also need to conduct member business at this meeting, which should not include the guests. What can you do? There are two ways to solve this.

First, you can invite guests at a prearranged time to follow the business meeting, and explain that they'll be arriving for the second portion of the meeting. Second, you may invite the guests and have their program first; an example might be if you want to honor local high school students and they must be home at a reasonable time on a school night. After their portion of the evening is over, explain that they will be excused for the business meeting.

 ESSENTIAL

Need to excuse your guests? If something comes up in a meeting and the group realizes that privacy must be maintained, a member can make a motion to go into executive session by declaring the open portion of the meeting ended, and guests can be excused.

Some groups find it easiest to have a separate meeting just for business. Other meetings then can be used for social programs or for other meetings. It all depends on what makes the most sense for your group.

Saving Time at Meetings

It's possible to make meetings more pleasant and more efficient using some commonsense rules. Mailing out an agenda ahead of time with any important information will help save time and make for better-informed members. (See Chapter 4 for more on agendas.) Check any equipment, such as audiovisual equipment, in advance to make certain that there are no problems. Start the meeting on time and don't allow latecomers to waste time by asking what's happened so far when they enter the meeting. Stay on schedule; if there is not a time limit for debate in your bylaws, set the rules for limits at the time of debate so that it doesn't drag on endlessly.

 ALERT!

It's tempting to limit the number of attendees at a meeting to save time—maybe even hold a special meeting to do this so something can be accomplished quickly. Be careful that this is not an attempt to limit participation by all members or your organization is treading on very nondemocratic ground!

Using Committees

Naming members to committees can save your organization time as well. A committee can meet separately and go over all the pros and cons of an issue. Then it can make a (brief!) report to the membership at a meeting and state its recommendation for action. Remember that by using committees, you are not attempting to eliminate debate; you simply get a smaller portion of the membership to conduct informed discussions on the issue and make a recommendation that will influence others, hopefully saving everyone time and energy.

Types of Committees

There are three types of committees: standing committees, select committees, and committees of the whole. The *standing committee* is a permanent one that is required by the bylaws. It can also be a committee appointed for a specific time or for a specific session.

A *select committee* operates temporarily and is established for a specific purpose, appointed, for instance, to study a particular issue (sometimes this committee is referred to as an ad hoc committee). It's dissolved after it does its work.

The third type, the *committee of the whole,* refers to the entire membership when it wants to work on a matter in a less structured, less formal way than it would in a meeting. This way, the membership acts as if it were a committee, dealing with the matter itself instead of referring it to a committee where it could become bogged down.

Committees can be used to draft or amend documents for the membership. They can write or amend constitutions and bylaws, and prepare motions that may be complicated, rules of order or business that are more specific to the organization, even charters (if they are necessary). They can also verify the voting credentials of members.

Committees for the Higher Good

Using committees also spreads out the power and influence among the membership. Committees allow individuals who aren't officers to serve and have a voice not only for themselves but also for other members. Of course, the use of committees isn't without problems. Selecting a committee can be tricky—too many like-minded individuals who agree with a chair's position, and they can be called the chair's yes-men. Too many dissenting members, and there can be a battle of wills.

Using General Consent

Use "general consent" to save time instead of taking votes on some issues. General consent means that the membership agrees that action can be taken by the organization. The chair should state, "If there is no objection, we will . . ." Then, if there is no objection, the chair should say, "Hearing no objection, we will . . ." And that's it.

General consent can be used to pay bills, to approve certain things such as the previous meeting's minutes, to consider committee reports and recommendations, to answer requests and correspondence—many, many noncontroversial matters. Using it can save a tremendous amount of time and hassle.

 QUESTION?

> **What if there is an objection to the general consent?**
> Then the action must be made into the form of a motion, seconded, put to a debate, and then voted upon. For more about making motions, see Chapter 6.

Tapping Leaders

Within a group or organization there are many people of diverse talents. Some might be interested in the specific, often legal language of bylaws and like to serve on the bylaws committee. Others might be better at social committees or planning committees. If you're a chair, get to know the strengths of individual members. Don't just use those with obvious skills, or those who have been asked to serve in the past.

As a leader, you should serve as a role model to encourage those who don't step forward because they're shy or insecure or feel inexperienced at serving in some capacity.

Have You Served?

If you're someone who has not stepped forward yet to offer your time and talents, think about the opportunity you're missing to contribute and have a voice in a group you're interested enough in to be a member. You may have the enthusiasm that some others are lacking, or a different approach that hasn't been tried yet. Whether you're male or female, a full-time parent and homemaker or employed outside the home, you can develop and polish skills that help you professionally as well as personally.

Keeping Things Moving

"New blood" is important to the health and well-being of any organization. Perhaps something's been tried before and it didn't work. It doesn't mean it can't succeed this time—some facet of the idea may be different. No organization is old because its members are; organizations become old by having the same old ideas and using the same old thinking over and over again—which can happen in a younger group, too! Using Robert's Rules isn't just about recognizing parliamentary procedure; it's about having a democratic organization that regards each member as a vital and necessary participant.

Are you presiding or presenting at a meeting, session, or convention? Learning what each is and some easy tips to save time and work more effectively will make you a valuable chair or presenter. Knowledgeable and efficient chairpersons and presenters are worth their weight in gold to members who have limited time and to groups and organizations that need the help of everyone to accomplish goals.

 ALERT!

> It bears repeating: Remember, no matter what type of meeting, how short the time, the chair and the membership should stay vigilant about the necessity of having a quorum at all times to conduct business. It's vital to the democratic aims of the group or organization!

Chapter 4
Getting Down to Business

Members are gathering and the time of the meeting is approaching. Everything is coming together. Preparation has met opportunity—the opportunity to further the aims and goals of your group or organization. Two important elements will keep the meeting focused and legal: an agenda and a quorum. The agenda is your structure for presentation of the business of the meeting; a quorum is the necessary number of members required to be present to transact legal business.

The Importance of a Quorum

Quorum may be the most important term in Robert's Rules. It means the minimum number of members of a group or organization who must be in attendance at a meeting in order to conduct any official business. No matter how the chair conducts a meeting, no matter what motions have been made, if a quorum is not present, business cannot be conducted. Period.

 ESSENTIAL

> Don't confuse the term *quorum* with the term *majority*. Quorum means the number of members who need to be present to legally transact business. A majority is the number of that quorum needed for an affirmative vote.

What's Your Number?

Your group wants to meet to discuss business and act on issues of importance, so you must decide from the beginning what constitutes a quorum. This quorum is necessary to prevent a few members from acting in ways that don't represent the majority of the members.

Sometimes a quorum is a majority of members; at other times, it is the number of people who can be expected to attend a meeting, except in unusual circumstances such as severe weather or other situations beyond their control. It's extremely important to put this quorum requirement in the bylaws, especially if the group is one that enacts legislation, gathers and spends a lot of money, and so on. It's also vital that the chair and all who attend make it a priority to be careful that a quorum exists *each time* a vote will be taken.

What is the number required for a quorum in your group or organization? Your bylaws should state the number for a quorum, but if such a requirement has not been made, Robert's Rules set out some specifics. In any meeting, a quorum is the number of enrolled members present. This is because they *are* the entire membership at the time.

In groups such as churches that have no required dues and no official list of members, a quorum consists of those who attend, as well. A quorum of delegates at a convention is simply the majority of the number of delegates who have registered to attend; even if some leave, there is still a quorum.

Avoiding Problems

Imagine this situation: Your group or organization doesn't have a quorum number specified in its bylaws. It numbers fifty members. At one evening's meeting, twenty people show up. Fifteen vote in favor of a motion you know most members are against. While there are ways to reverse this vote, it's going to cause a lot of work and ruffle a lot of feathers to do so. How much simpler it would have been to specify a quorum.

It's Your Job, Too

It must be the job of everyone, not just the chair, to make certain that a quorum is present at all times that a vote is to be taken during the meeting. If you're the chair, do your research before a meeting to determine what is a quorum for your group. (Some groups even specify within their bylaws the number that is the quorum.)

Then, throughout the meeting, try to do a brief scan of the room to see if there appears to be enough members to take a vote; some presiding officers will take a head count before the vote, just in case. Ultimately, it's the responsibility of every member to make certain that a quorum exists when business is transacted for it to be legal. If there is no quorum, a member should raise a point of order (see Chapter 9).

 QUESTION?

What if you have a quorum, then members leave?
Bring the matter to the attention of the chair. Otherwise, all actions taken by the group in the absence of a quorum are considered invalid.

Gathering a Quorum

You've received the agenda for the next meeting and note that a matter that is very important to you—or important to your group or organization—is on it. Maybe you support the idea for a fundraiser so more charitable work can be done in the community. Perhaps a decision needs to be made on naming scholarship recipients. Voting is to take place on a slate of officers and you're hoping that there will be new leadership, not another year of *that* chair. What can you do to ensure voting will happen and business will be valid?

Burn up Those Wires

It's time to get out that phone list of members. You do have a phone list of members, don't you? If your group or organization is large, divide up the list with other interested members, and start calling. You want to call as many members as you can to make certain that there will be not only a quorum for the meeting, but the number of members required for an affirmative vote.

Send up the Smoke Signals

An alternative to making phone calls is to e-mail or fax other members to make certain that they know that an important item will be on the agenda at your group or organization meeting. Keep the message as brief as possible while emphasizing the importance of their attendance at the meeting for passage of the motion. Include your phone number in case they want more information.

Be prepared for people to let you know they aren't in favor of your pet project. You can hope that they'll either change their minds after they hear debate or be outvoted. Or better yet, that they'll stay home. It's okay as long as you have a quorum.

In the Absence of a Quorum

Where'd everybody go? You're sitting at a meeting and suddenly you realize that your quorum is no longer present. Perhaps people have been drifting out quietly (tiptoeing out early to catch that game on TV?). The matter that was being discussed was so interesting, maybe you weren't fully aware that people were getting up and leaving. What can you do now? You might not like the answer: not a lot.

 FACT

> Sometimes you may notice there's no quorum after a motion has been made. If there was no quorum at the time it was proposed, it's invalid. It's as if it never happened at all. The motion should be introduced again at the next meeting as new business.

What Can Be Done?

The only business that can be taken care of is to fix the time to which to adjourn, adjourn, and recess (see Chapter 8). Or, the group or organization can take steps to obtain a quorum. The members present could vote for a recess, and then call members who are absent and see if they can attend. In a few instances, some legislative bodies have the legal authority to have absent members brought to their meetings. But that's probably not your group or organization!

Keep It Legal

It can't be stressed enough that groups and organizations can't transact business without a quorum. This rule can't be waived even by unanimous consent, or with previous notice. If it's required that a meeting be conducted at a particular time and there's no quorum, the meeting can convene, but then it must adjourn.

But We Have to Act Now!

If there is business that needs to be conducted and there is no quorum, members should fix the time for an adjourned meeting and then adjourn. But in an emergency, there is one "out": Members who are present can go ahead and take care of the emergency in the hope that when the group or organization meets next (and has a quorum), the members will approve and ratify their actions.

 ESSENTIAL

The number of members needed to take action in a committee or board is the majority of its members, unless the entire membership or bylaws says otherwise. Sometimes the entire membership will decide to meet as a committee of the whole. When it does, the quorum is the number of all members.

Changing Quorum Requirements

Sometimes it's hard to get a quorum at your meetings. Perhaps your area has been having unusually bad weather. Or the opposite—it's summer, and everyone wants to be at the beach. Some communities may have a large influx of attendees at a club during the winter months, then the "snowbirds" depart north when the weather gets hot. There can be disinterest on the part of the members for a wide variety of reasons. Your group still needs to transact business, but the quorum minimum in the bylaws is ironclad. Or is it?

Nothing's Written in Stone

Quorum requirements *can* be changed. It's not something for members of a group or organization to take lightly, but it may become necessary. While sometimes extreme disinterest can signal that the time for a group or organization has passed and its demise is imminent, this may not be true. It is probably possible to convince members that something needs to be done to keep the group alive.

Making the Change

Has your group decided a change should be made in quorum requirements, permitting a smaller number of members to decide matters? Proceed cautiously here. A member should propose striking out the old requirement and inserting the new requirement at the same time; the membership should then vote on this as one question (motion). An example of the motion might be, "I move that we strike out the old requirement for a quorum and insert the number [XX] as the required quorum."

If the group or organization doesn't proceed this way, it could find itself in a kind of quicksand here. If members take out the old rule without implementing a new number at the same time, then a majority of the membership becomes the quorum. That number will be larger than what you're trying to get rid of, because a quorum is the total number of members in most cases—remember?

 ALERT!

Consult your bylaws to see what requirements there are for changing bylaws. There may be language specifying that there be previous notice sent out and two-thirds of the membership must approve a bylaw change.

The Order of Business

Deciding on the order of your meeting is crucial. It can help save time, always an important consideration. More importantly, the proper sequence and amount of time is given to matters most important to the group. Busy members will agree that they do not want to sit around and listen to long discussions on trivial issues.

Agenda Basics

An agenda is the accepted order of business—a program of business to be conducted at your meeting. Its purpose is to make the handling of the group's business an orderly process, based on the first principle of parliamentary procedure, which is to take up one item at a time.

An agenda is prepared well ahead of the meeting. It is often distributed ahead of time to its members by mail, e-mail, or fax; distribution is sometimes mandatory in certain groups. If you are in charge of an agenda, spend the time to think it through and refine it carefully. A good agenda will save a lot of time and effort and make things run smoothly at your meeting.

Some groups follow an agenda to the letter; other groups choose to be flexible, changing things as the meeting proceeds. It's especially important to have an agenda set for meetings that occur only a few times a year, and for conventions or conferences, so everything can be accomplished. Even if your group adopts an agenda before the meeting (which requires a majority vote), the agenda can be changed with a two-thirds vote at any time during the meeting.

Typical Order of Business

A particular order of business (another name for an agenda) won't always work for all organizations. However, a general format may be helpful to use as a springboard. Here is a typical order (note that calling the meeting to order and adjournment aren't considered part of the order of business):

1. Reading and approval of minutes
2. Reports by officers, boards, committees
3. Reports by special committees
4. Special orders
5. Unfinished business and general orders
6. New business

 ESSENTIAL

Unless your group or organization is brand-new, it likely has an established format for an agenda. It's probably been developed with a lot of trial and error during many meetings. Use the format that works for your group's needs.

How the Order of Business Works

The adoption of Robert's Rules by so many organizations has provided chairs, members, and the general public with an orderly, familiar way of running meetings. Think about how many times you've attended meetings of diverse groups and yet known how they would operate because they have adopted Robert's Rules. Reading the minutes comes first, and justifiably so—they are the official record of a meeting, and making certain they are accurate is the job of all, not just the job of the secretary.

Then, too, members who missed the last meeting can hear a quick synopsis and catch up.

Reports by the various officers, boards, and committee members follow. These elected or appointed officeholders have the responsibility of sharing important information pertaining to their office or the task they've been given.

General orders are those that a majority vote has decided will be acted upon at a specific meeting; this has been done by postponement, adoption of an agenda, or a main motion. Special orders are adopted by a two-thirds vote and a main motion that has the words *special order* attached to it. Special orders have a specific priority or time at which they will be discussed, and at which action will be taken upon them. The matter should be dealt with at that assigned time and should come before other matters before the group.

 FACT

The chair has the responsibility of making certain that general and special orders are taken care of at the time assigned. If she does not do this, a member should call it to the attention of the group so that action can be taken.

Next, unfinished business is dealt with. Sometimes there is such a sheer volume of business to be handled at a meeting that not all of it can be accomplished. Other times, it may be that there was an extended discussion and so some business from a previous meeting was brought forward to be finished at the current meeting.

New business is just that—this is the first time it will come to the attention of the board. A longer, more in-depth discussion of this will be featured in a later chapter, but for now, it's enough to say that new business can catch the attention of those who want the organization that is meeting to be active and vital in approaching new ways to conduct its business and further its aims.

 ESSENTIAL

> As the leader of an organization, you'll soon see that there will be members who do not have the same depth of knowledge of the rules of order as you and others do. It's impor-tant to foster an atmosphere where diplo-macy, as well as attention to rules, reigns.

Creating an Agenda

How do you decide what to put on the agenda? Before the meeting date, the chair or secretary should mail, e-mail, or fax a notice to members that asks them to respond with new items they wish to have brought before the membership. There are groups that require members to notify the secretary about new business in writing. These items can be added to the agenda under either new or unfinished business (sometimes called "old" business).

The minutes of the previous meeting should also be consulted to see what needs to be brought forward. Is there unfinished business to put on the agenda? Were any motions pending at the time of adjournment? Are there special orders or motions that have been postponed to this meeting? Are there any nominations or elections? Are there new members who need to be voted in? Are there any general orders?

It can be an interesting tightrope walk learning how much business, new and old, can reasonably be conducted in a meeting. Experience is the best guide. Whether you're a longtime member or a new one, experienced with running meetings or new to the challenge, asking others for their advice about your group and its needs regarding an agenda is always a good idea.

 ESSENTIAL

Whether new business has been put on the agenda or not, most chairs will ask the membership at a meeting if there is any new business. Members have the right to present their ideas about what the group should do, at the time that new business is discussed.

There are a number of styles for agendas, depending on what works best for your group or organization. Here are some sample preliminary agendas your group or organization might use:

- Reading, correction, and approval of minutes of previous meeting
- Officers' reports (such as from the treasurer)
- Executive committee report
- Standing committee reports (such as membership)
- Special committee reports (such as annual convention or conference)
- Unfinished business (sometimes called "old" business)
- New business
- Announcements

Another group or organization might use an agenda that looks like this:

- Reading and approval of minutes
- Reports of officers, boards, and standing committees
- Reports of special (select or ad hoc) committees
- Special orders
- Unfinished business and general orders
- New business

Some organizations that are fraternal or more social might choose the rather formal style shown below:

- Opening ceremonies or exercises (Pledge of Allegiance or prayer/invocation)
- Roll call

- Good of the order (or general good and welfare)*
- Announcements
- Program (good of the order is sometimes considered a program)

This is a general discussion about the work of the organization, announcements, and so on (not business or motions).

 FACT

> The term *program* is often used to list events such as informative or entertainment talks or lectures, films, and so on outside the business meeting. It can be included with the agenda or order of business for the meeting or convention.

Consent and Priority Agendas

A group may use a consent agenda, which enables members to vote on a block of items that are noncontroversial without a lot of time or discussion. If the group usually doesn't have any problem approving the minutes, paying bills, and other official business, this may be the way to go.

To use a consent agenda, each member must receive a copy before the start of the meeting. A consent agenda doesn't mean you have to approve everything on it to use it; members can request that an item be "extracted" (removed). No second or vote is necessary for the removal.

After any items are removed, the chair can either use general consent or take a vote. Since a group that is amenable to a consent agenda probably won't object, the chair should say: "If there is no objection, the consent agenda will be adopted. Hearing no objection, the items on your consent agenda are adopted." If there is an objection, the chair should proceed to a vote.

 QUESTION?

Where do the removed items go?
Any business that the membership removed from the consent agenda should be placed on the regular agenda. It will be dealt with as any item of business would in the category in which it belongs (new business, unfinished business, and so on). A member or members have simply indicated that they prefer to have the item(s) up for discussion and a vote.

A priority agenda is all about how important a matter is to the members. Each task is taken up in order of importance. This agenda is good for organizing a meeting, especially for committees and small groups that, because of their informality, might get off track and not get everything done. A priority agenda can also be used under the new business category on any agenda;

listing items in the order of their importance can ensure that they're taken care of in a timely manner.

Orders of the Day

An order of the day is that item of business that has been previously scheduled to be brought up at a specific time, meeting, and date. The only time something different can then take precedence is if other business has more importance *or* if the membership votes to set it aside when its time to come up arrives. However, an order of the day can't be taken up before the time it's set for unless a motion to reconsider the vote is made (and possible) or the rules are suspended by a two-thirds vote of the membership. There are general orders and special orders.

General Orders

General orders are any questions (motions) that have been made an order of the day because of postponement. Under the agenda heading of "Unfinished Business and General Orders," you might find the question that was pending when the previous meeting was adjourned and any questions that were unfinished business items at the previous meeting.

General orders might also be any questions that were made general orders because they weren't completed at the previous meeting, and anything that was set as a general order for the upcoming meeting. The general orders should be taken up in the order just listed.

ALERT!

While the chair will, in most cases, ask the membership if there is new business, it is not customary to ask if there is unfinished business. It can make for just too much disruption in a meeting.

Special Orders

A special order is an order of the day made with the provision that any rules that might interfere with its being taken up will be suspended except for adjournment or recess, questions of privilege, special orders made before *this* special order, or a question that has priority by being made the most important special order of the day. Since the making of a special order in effect suspends rules that interfere, it requires a two-thirds vote.

Sometimes a special order is business that is addressed once a year, such as nominations and elections. The only way it can't be taken care of at the time prescheduled is if something else is more important and takes precedence over it.

If a member feels a matter is important and wants to make certain that it is addressed at a particular meeting (perhaps to make certain he or she can get those who agree in attendance at the meeting), it's easy to make it a special order. The process is made by making a simple motion. The member should say: "I move that [the matter] be made a special order for [the time and date of the next meeting]."

Calling the Meeting to Order/ Adjourning

Finally, it's time to call the meeting to order. The agenda is prepared. The members have arrived. It's time to begin.

Heading Them Up

The chair should call the meeting to order by saying, "The meeting will come to order." A simple, "Will the members be seated so the meeting can begin" is often enough to gather a small group and start the meeting. Then, the chair can say, "This meeting will come to order." Using a gavel is optional for the chair. Sometimes that's a bit too formal in a small group.

Moving Them Out

And you're done; it's time to adjourn the meeting. Whether it has been a short or long meeting, many important matters have probably been taken care of—or postponed to another meeting. Sometimes a quorum is present and business can be conducted. Other times, a quorum isn't present from the time the meeting should begin, and the meeting must be adjourned immediately. A member might rise and make a motion to adjourn, or there may be a fixed time to adjourn.

So, for however long or short your meeting might be, a member can make a motion to adjourn by saying, "I move that the meeting adjourn." Another member seconds it. There is no debate. A majority vote decides the meeting is adjourned. The chair announces this in the same way that he announces the result of other votes ("The yeas have it"), and says, "The meeting is adjourned."

 ESSENTIAL

> The chair can also adjourn the meeting. If you're the chair, you can ask, "Is there any further business?" If there is none, the chair can simply say, "If there is no objection, the meeting will adjourn." Then, if no one says anything, "Since there is no objection, the meeting is adjourned."

Using Robert's Rules can make meetings easier for those who preside over them and the members who participate in them. Some careful planning will ensure that the business that the group or organization wants to conduct will be orderly, democratic, and efficient. Attention to rules such as quorum requirements, special scheduling requirements (such as orders of the day), and knowing when to adjourn will make your meetings successful and, hopefully, enjoyable!

Chapter 5
Types of Motions

Motions are the tools that make things happen at your meetings. There are many different types of motions: main motions, motions to open a question to debate, motions to end debate, motions to call a member to order, motions to reconsider motions, motions to postpone, motions to adjourn . . . well, you get the idea. Don't panic—you don't have to learn every one of them. In this chapter, we'll hit the high points of the most often used motions and explain them.

Classification of Motions

Since a motion is a powerful tool to make things happen, it's important to use the correct motion and to word it the best that you can. This doesn't mean that you have to sound like a senator or a parliamentarian, but that you watch your words and use the right motion for the right action you desire.

Motions were neatly classified by Robert in his Rules of Order. First and most important are the main motions, which include the original ones made by members and also the incidental main motions. Next in line are the secondary motions, which include subsidiary, privileged, and incidental motions. Finally, there are the motions that bring the question under consideration back to the forefront after a debate.

Why Classify the Motions?

It's important to classify the motions to better understand their order and importance. For example, a business has its president, vice president, and so on down the hierarchy. The main motion is like the president, holding the most importance, and everything should be done with the idea of serving the main motion. So, just as the vice president and others assist the president in achieving the goals of the company, so the motions classified beneath the main motion should assist its goal.

Let's say that the group has been looking for a way to raise funds. A member makes a motion to consider a fund-raising opportunity. There is discussion by the membership. Then another member might make a motion to have that original member do more research and get back to the group. This would be an example of an incidental motion—it serves the original motion.

In the Beginning . . .

Here's the order of making motions:

- First the main motion is made.
- That main motion may be postponed indefinitely, amended, or referred to a committee.
- There could be a motion to limit or extend limits or debate.
- Members could move on the previous question (vote on the motion).
- There can be a motion to lay the original motion on the table.
- Someone could call for the orders of the day if they have been scheduled at this particular time.
- A question of privilege could be raised. ("The room is too warm," and so on. See Chapter 8.)
- There could be a call for a recess.
- There could be a motion to adjourn.
- Someone could want to fix the time to adjourn (so the meeting doesn't run over).

Now for the Voting

The order of voting on motions is the reverse of the above list. Members would vote on these motions in this order:

- Fix the time to which to adjourn
- Adjourn
- Recess
- Question of privilege
- Call for the orders of the day
- Lay on the table
- Previous question
- Limit or extend limits of debate
- Postpone to a certain time
- Refer to a committee
- Amend
- Postpone indefinitely
- The original main motion

An Important Rule to Remember

Some people think that there cannot be more than one motion being considered at a time. This isn't true. A main motion can be proposed, and another motion can be made to amend it. So then there are two motions on the floor.

Confused? Don't be. Just remember that *only motions that further the main motion can be considered*. A secondary motion might be to reword the main motion, to refer it to a committee for study, to place a time constraint on debate, and so on. If a member seconds the motion, it may then be debated and voted upon. Just remember that motions can't be made to address a new matter or digress into other areas while a main motion is before the membership. A more detailed explanation of main motions is located in Chapter 6, but for now, this serves as a good introduction to the important points.

 FACT

> People often think that it's okay to attach changes or unrelated motions to a main motion because the U.S. Congress often passes bills with unrelated amendments attached. This is not allowed under Robert's Rules. Motions may be amended by their maker, but no unrelated wordage may be applied to a motion.

The Main Motion

This is the most important element of parliamentary procedure that powers your meeting. The main motion often sets the tone for the meeting; it can be the focus of an entire meeting depending on how important it is and how much debate is necessary. Never rush something as important as a main motion.

Think of the main motion as the main course of a meal—it's the part that really is most important to you, and other things accompany it without being the focus.

The business of the organization is served by motions or resolutions (made with a motion) that create and regulate the actions of the organization and authorize the spending of its funds.

How to Make a Motion

To make a motion, a member should request the floor. She does this by rising and addressing the chair. After the chair acknowledges that the member has the floor—usually by addressing the member by name—the member should say, "I move that [content of motion]." An example might be, "I move that we spend $1,000 to send the chair and one committee member to the national conference this year."

Then a second member must second the motion to send it to debate and a vote. A motion is always considered if two people are in support of its coming before the meeting, unless a motion has been made by a committee. If the committee has made a motion, it's assumed that at least two people have been in favor of its going before the group.

Is There a Second?

After the motion has been made, a member who is in agreement seconds it. Let's assume for now that there is a second to the motion. The chair should restate the motion before the matter is debated, and also again before there is a vote. If the motion is long and complex, it's best to put it in writing to be read aloud—and, if it's a very important matter, even have copies made so that it can be passed around to the membership. After debate, a vote is taken. If the member who proposed the motion feels the need to amend the motion, he or she may do so. Voting against your own motion is allowed after debate, but speaking against it in debate is a no-no!

No Seconds?

What if no one seconds the motion? Then the chair should say, "As there is no second, the motion is not before the meeting." Obviously, if a motion is important to its maker, finding out ahead of time if there is support or opposition to it is important. Speaking out and trying to enlist the membership to support something or spend funds on an issue of importance should always be done, but first it may be a good idea to scope out the lay of the land and find out if it's worth your time to proceed. If you have support, you know that someone will second your motion and then debate can be entered into.

 ESSENTIAL

A member who proposes a motion may withdraw the motion unless there is an objection from the membership. The chair simply states that if there is no objection, the motion is withdrawn.

Accomplishing the Purpose of the Motion

Obviously, you're hoping to accomplish something with your main motion. You want your group to take action on a matter of importance to you and the membership. It's important to be clear and word what you want done in positive terms, such as, "I move that the XYZ Condominium Association support the expansion of Highway 19" instead of saying, "I move that we oppose the bill to block the expansion of Highway 19" because it's easy for such motions to be misunderstood or confused.

I Second That!

After all is said and done, a main motion requires a second. This is to be done by someone other than the person who made the original main motion. As stated previously, it can be debated, amended, postponed, and so on, but when things come full circle—the times and terms of debate have been exhausted—and action is required, a seconding motion needs to be made.

At this point, a member should make a motion to "move the previous question." This might sound a bit strange, but all it means is that the member is making a motion to stop debate and have a vote taken on the original motion. It's wise to have the chair note this to the membership and call for a vote. To stop debate, there must be a two-thirds majority vote of the membership. Most parliamentarians suggest that those in favor and then those opposed should demonstrate this with a show of hands (if a small group) or by standing (if it's a large group), instead of using voices to vote ("aye" or "no"). This is because it's sometimes hard to hear if it's a majority or just a small number of members who are being loud.

If a two-thirds vote is in favor of stopping debate, then it's on to the actual vote on the motion (which, of course, also requires a majority). Remember, a majority is whatever your group's bylaws state that it is.

When Things Can't Be Changed

A main motion can't change something that has already been adopted, such as the bylaws. If these could be changed at every meeting, imagine the chaos that could arise! If your group has put into effect special rules of order, these also can't be changed at a regular meeting. These are especially important rules for all organizations.

 QUESTION?

Are you sorry you made that motion?
If a motion seems like a really bad idea for some reason, another member of the group can make a motion to *postpone* the matter indefinitely.

Bringing New Business to a Meeting

Although many groups choose to discuss new business after unfinished business and other matters, it's important to remember that your group can bring new business to the meeting in whatever order is most appropriate for it. The bylaws should reflect whatever your individual group finds is the best order for its meetings. Some organizations find that they do not bring a lot of unfinished business to a meeting, usually taking care of whatever matter is before them and starting off with a generally clean slate. For them, starting with new business works best.

Hot off the Press!

Some new business can also be conducted in a simpler way. Routine business can be accomplished simply by the chair's specifying an action and announcing that if there is no objection, the action is considered adopted. The chair would say, "There being no objection, the action is adopted." This is called general or unanimous consent. If a member does object, then the formal process discussed earlier (a formal motion, a second, debate, and then a vote on the motion) should be used.

Business can also be transacted by communications. During the meeting, when a member or the chair of a committee gives a report, a member can introduce business in the form of a written communication. This could be a faxed memo or letter or an e-mail or a videoconference or teleconference. The chair or secretary (or clerk) should read the communication to the membership. Then, if any member wishes the group to consider the content of the communication, it must be put into the form of a motion by a member.

 ALERT!

In an urgent situation when the chair is suddenly given a written communication in a meeting, she should always privately read it before sharing it aloud with the membership. This is to make certain it doesn't contain sensitive or confidential information that should not be shared with everyone.

We Resolve

A motion to take action isn't the only way an organization conducts its business. Sometimes a member can propose a resolution—a statement that the organization is in favor of or opposed to a matter. Often resolutions are more formal and complex and are written down and presented for a vote by members. The resolution must then be seconded and voted upon. Then it can be debated by the members.

An example of a resolution might be for a city council to name a day for a civic leader or celebrity. A council member would write a resolution and either read it to the council and its audience or pass it to the chair to read. The member might say, "I move the adoption of the following resolution: Resolved, that August 10 be named Jane Wright Day, in honor of the many contributions this former councilwoman made to our city." If the resolution is very lengthy, the member might say, "I move the assembly approve the resolution relating to [and summarize the resolution], which I have given to the chair." If the resolution is offered to the chair to read, he or she would introduce the resolution by saying, "The resolution offered by [member's name] is as follows. . . . "

 ESSENTIAL

> Resolutions are a great way for a civic organization to show support for—or raise a warning flag of caution about—a local issue such as a tax increase for schools or a fund drive. The support can sometimes be even more valuable than a monetary contribution.

Staying Focused

Don't let the meeting degenerate into trivial discussions of minor issues. You'll lose members to either boredom or the chance to duck out early, pleading other commitments, and there will go your quorum. Likewise, don't allow important discussions to become sidetracked by nitpickers who want to parade their alleged superior knowledge of parliamentary procedure or those who begin to ponderously detail the history of the group whenever someone wants to do something new. Leaders should lead, and in the absence of focused effective leadership, someone—you, if you're not the leader—should try to get the group back on track in a courteous, proper way.

 ALERT!

Sometimes people use the term *table a motion,* but this term is incorrect. The chair should ask if the member wants to kill the motion or postpone it to another meeting. If the answer is to kill it, the chair should rule the motion out of order. If it's to postpone, the motion should be reworded to say so.

If Things Go Astray

If, during discussion, someone takes the floor to add to a motion, the chair should remind the speaker and the membership that amendments to the original motion can't be made at this time. This doesn't mean that the chair has to rebuke the speaker. The request can be politely phrased and debate continued. Only after debate is completed and the motion has been voted upon can a member add to the motion.

When Interruptions Are Allowed

Interruptions are allowed when there is a call for the orders of the day—a request made for the agenda to be followed or when a prearranged time to debate an issue has been set for some other time. It is also all right for a member to make a point of order, such as when there has been a breach in the rules of the meeting. If there is something that is interfering with the rights of an individual or the group, it is correct to interrupt. Perhaps there is an urgent need to address something happening in the meeting that affects the comfort or safety of a member or the group.

 ESSENTIAL

> To make a motion to object to the consideration of a motion, a member should say, "I object to the consideration of the question." This objection can't be debated, amended, or have any motion such as a subsidiary motion attached to it.

Also, if a confidential matter is being discussed and a member believes it shouldn't be discussed before a guest or the press, it is correct to interrupt to bring this to the chair's attention. Finally, a member can interrupt to make a motion to reconsider a motion. A member can stop debate on an issue by making a motion to object to the consideration of the question. A vote must take place on this, and if a two-thirds majority agrees with the motion, debate is effectively stopped.

It's Decided

Once a group has made a decision on an issue, any attempts to undermine it by making motions contrary to it should be discouraged by ruling them out of order. Some people may have trouble handling the fact that their opinions on a matter aren't those of the majority. But once the majority has voted, discontented members can't be allowed the opportunity to undo what has been decided. These attempts should always be firmly addressed by the chair.

Give Me Some Notice!

An agenda should be prepared before the meeting and sent to the membership with enough time for the members to study it. This job is done by the group's secretary. A notice can be mailed, e-mailed, or faxed depending on the preference of the group. The technology of e-mail and faxing has been a boon to many groups because of the speed of delivery and the savings on postage, photocopying, paper, and workload. (Not everyone has a computer and Internet access, however, so notices must still be mailed to those who prefer hard copies.)

Who Gets Notified?

Officers and the membership should get copies of the agenda. Additional copies should be available at the meeting for those who don't bring their copies. You'll find that having a copy of the agenda on hand will save time and keep things on track.

Is It in the Bylaws?

Your group should have language in its bylaws that details when regular meetings are to be scheduled and how special meetings may be called. The bylaws should also detail how members are to be notified. This keeps things "legal" and prevents members with devious intentions from not notifying others when they want to conduct secret meetings. (Most organizations do not allow verbal notice.)

If yours is an established group, check your bylaws. If yours is a new group, incorporate what is best for your members and goals in your bylaws. Do your bylaws say if an agenda is to be sent to members and by what date before a meeting? Do the bylaws specify notification by mail? Is e-mail or fax acceptable? How much notice is required? One day's notice? A week's? How much notice is required for any meetings or sessions that are not regularly scheduled? How do members schedule time on the agenda? Is notice to the public required? Are nonmembers allowed to be at the meeting?

 ALERT!

The principle underlying Robert's Rules is that individual and majority rights are always to be protected by parliamentary procedure in an organization; whatever is democratic and serves the organization is what you should use when in doubt about how to notify members or conduct any business in your group.

Whether you're a chair or a presenter, motions are the tools you'll use to conduct business for your group or organization. Craftsmen learn through experience which tool to use for the job, and you, too, will find that through experience, you'll know which motion will do the job you want. Think of the most common motions list of motions available in Appendix B as your toolkit for successful meetings, and keep it handy for quick reference.

Now that you have a better overall idea of the way Robert's Rules operates in a meeting situation, it's time for more specifics. In this chapter, you'll learn a little more about the main motion. Some examples of main motions are offered to help guide you as you prepare to lead or present at a meeting. Main motions sometimes become the main business of a meeting, so their importance cannot be overstated. But don't be intimidated—this chapter will make them easy for you!

The Main Event

A main motion is the only motion that introduces new business at the meeting of a group or organization. One main motion can become the central focus of an entire meeting if the motion is important enough to the membership. It can become, as stated earlier in this book, like the main course of a meal. Some examples of main motions that can be the entire focus of a meeting include a PTA deciding on what its fundraising activity will be that year or how to spend the funds that are received at that activity, or a volunteer firefighting group considering the ramifications of a motion requiring them to get more education on their own time. A motion to raise the minimum age requirement to live in an adult community might take an entire evening—or more—for a homeowner's association to debate. Main motions often involve weighty issues.

Making Things Happen

Main motions are formal proposals that bring attention to a matter by their introduction, or they may be offered after a report or communication is presented. The maker of a main motion hopes for some action, but this doesn't necessarily mean a physical action; other actions can also be to state a particular view or send the study of an issue to a committee. Main motions must stand on their own in terms of content although other motions such as subsidiary and incidental motions can assist them.

Because they're so important, main motions deserve and should get a lot of attention. If you're the presenter of a main motion, it's important that you do all that you can to present your motion professionally. Main motions that are long or complicated are often presented in writing to the chair and the membership. Before offering a main motion in writing, word it carefully and proofread it even more carefully, then have someone else look it over. (Think about having photocopies of it available for interested members.)

 ESSENTIAL

If you know in advance that you'll be making a main motion, you might want to have a friend or associate listen to it.

The member who makes a motion can modify his own motion before it is stated by the chair. It's even permissible to modify the motion after it's stated by the chair. The member can have a change of heart and withdraw the motion up until the time the chair states it, but after that, the membership must give permission for withdrawal.

Who Makes a Main Motion?

The best part of it all, the reason you're in a group or organization and reading this book, is the pure democratic ideal that is the basis of Robert's Rules, and, in a greater sense, this country. Every member (with the exception of the president, serving as chair), regardless of personal or professional connections or background, has a right to make a main motion. (Guests, of course, can't make motions.) This doesn't mean that a member should make a main motion for trivial reasons, or with ulterior motives, but that there is an equal playing field for all to contribute. And who knows what contribution even the most unlikely person might make?

 FACT

Are you an active member of your group? Some groups and organizations do not allow members who don't attend regularly to participate or vote. This encourages a more active membership. Check to see what the rules are for your group.

Main Motions Introducing New Business

It's important to take another look at how to make a motion. The procedure is simple, but this step is so important to the success of what you want, it bears another look.

Timing is important. You don't want to make a motion at a time when members won't be receptive, nor do you want to propose action on something too far in the distance—or too late to be effective for your purposes. Once the timing is right, you're ready to make the motion.

You've asked someone to give you advice on your motion or even put it into writing and maybe made copies to have available for members. Next, at the appropriate time, you'll request the floor by rising and addressing the chair. Once you've been acknowledged, you should state your motion verbally by saying, "I move that [your motion happen]." An example might be, "I move that we spend $5,000 to start a scholarship fund for fraternity members who give a hundred hours of service to the community each year."

Hopefully, you have other members in support of this idea, because you'll need someone to second the motion so that there can then be debate on it. The debate will be in accordance with whatever you've previously put in your group or organization bylaws. Your bylaws could make it possible to act on the motion at that meeting, but it's hoped your group will wait until the next meeting. You don't want members to feel that they did not get a chance to speak.

Putting It to Vote

People often miss something that's been said. Maybe they were chatting with a neighbor, or their mind was on their busy day and the errands they still need to do. For whatever reason, they just aren't always "there" when they need to be. So it's always a good idea for the chair to restate the motion before it's debated and again before the membership votes. That way, there can be no misunderstanding.

If you realize that the motion isn't worded as it should have been, as the maker of the motion you may ask the chair to let you amend it before it goes to debate. During debate, the membership can also make a motion to amend your motion (and this will require a second and a vote).

Once it is time to vote, the membership can vote on whether they want a majority to decide whether the motion passes or fails, or if they prefer a two-thirds vote for it to pass.

 ESSENTIAL

> The maker of a motion may vote against her own motion but may not debate against it during the debate process. If you decide your motion is a bad idea, amend it or withdraw it, but don't confuse people or waste their time—or show that you're conflicted!

If at First You Don't Succeed . . .

Uh-oh. The chair has just said, "As there is no second, the motion is not before the meeting." Sad to say, no matter how much you prepared, or thought you had a finger on the pulse of what your group or organization needs, no one wanted to second your motion.

Or, perhaps worse, the membership has voted against your motion.

There can, of course, be as many reasons for its failure as there are members. But in any case, it just didn't "go." What should you do? Be gracious. Subside. Don't argue or attempt to persuade or bring up the matter again at that meeting. Definitely don't glower at others—even those who might have indicated beforehand that they'd support you if you stuck your neck out with such a motion!

Remember that while you can't reintroduce the motion at that meeting, there is always the next meeting. Maybe by that time others will realize that your motion was a good one and be more amenable. Or you may just have to bide your time until some point in the future. After all, timing is everything. As a wise person once said, "A rejection is just a rejection of that particular thing by that particular person or group at that particular time. Next time might be the right time!" If you believe in what you proposed, don't be discouraged. Learn from the experience and move on.

"Secondhand" Motions

Are you interested in making a second attempt at your motion? It's not allowed at the same meeting (unless your group's or organization's rules specifically allow it), but it is permissible at the next (and the next . . . not that we're suggesting that you make a pest of yourself).

When a motion is presented again in its same form, it's called a renewal of motion.

If you feel you've learned something from the debate before it was voted down, and you've substantially reworded it, you should indicate this at the meeting so that it won't be mistaken for a renewal of motion. (Graciousness on your part can go a long way toward showing what kind of individual you are and, not so incidentally, can lead to the success of your motion as well!)

 ALERT!

> Main motions can't be renewed if they've been referred to a committee for study. This would essentially be taking away the ability of the committee to do its work. If you haven't been appointed to the committee, ask if you can appear before it to present your views for consideration.

Who Proposes Motions?

Besides coming from individual members, main motions can originate from a few other sources. Sometimes the business of a group or organization is "prepped" by a committee. Members of a committee can help save others a lot of time and energy and, more importantly, allow those who have some special expertise to oversee the preparation of documents and other business. If, after the committee has studied a matter for some time, it offers a motion to the membership, that motion is often considered more seriously than if it had been proposed by an individual member.

 FACT

> Unlike the group or organization chair (president), the chair of a committee may make motions and vote during committee meetings over which she presides.

An additional time-saver comes with the making of a motion by a committee: A main motion made by a committee does not require a second. (While this doesn't translate into a huge savings of time, in a long meeting, every little bit helps!) This not only prevents the need for someone to make a motion to second, but it also helps the motion attain more importance *because* it doesn't require a second.

Motions from Communications

Main motions can arise from the reading of communications at a meeting of a group or organization. For example, the national executive board of the local chapter of your group could send a letter urging your members to host the next national convention. A high school could write a fraternity asking for help mentoring students and raising funds for computers. Or a political action committee urges your group to support a moratorium on new building in the area.

It's not necessary to make a motion to receive the communication. The chair or secretary simply announces that a communication has been received and it will be read aloud to the membership. Then a member can make a motion in favor of or in opposition to the content of the communication, someone can second it, and debate and a vote follow—or the motion can die for lack of a second—the same procedure as with any other main motion.

ESSENTIAL

It's not necessary to make a motion to receive a committee report. The usual procedure is for committee reports to be placed on an agenda, and the chair will call for the committee to present its report at the appropriate time.

Main Motions from Previous Actions

There are other ways that a main motion can come before a group or organization. A main motion could come up automatically at a particular time without anyone making a motion right at that moment if it's been previously postponed until this meeting. A special order could also have designated a particular time during this meeting for the main motion to be brought up, and the chair announces it at the meeting. Then the usual procedure (a member seconds it, debate and a vote follow, or the motion dies for lack of a second) takes place just as if the main motion had just been made.

Remember the Resolutions

Main motions can be resolutions, as mentioned briefly earlier. Never discount the value of a resolution. Your group might not have the funds to support a particular issue or event, but it can send a message with a resolution that says your membership is behind its aims. A resolution can be in the form of thanking someone or some group for doing something to better the community. Its possibilities are endless and the resolution costs nothing (except perhaps a minimal cost to print up a letter or fancy-looking proclamation to announce it!).

 FACT

> A resolution is a form of a main motion so it is dealt with in the same way as a main motion is. It must have a second unless it has been made by a committee, and it can be amended, debated, and voted upon.

We Interrupt This Motion to Say . . .

It's important to interrupt here with a cautionary note—while the *content* of main motions is usually extremely important to a group or organization, other motions—privileged, incidental, and subsidiary—take precedence over it. Confused? It's easy to be.

Briefly, privileged motions are important motions such as fix the time to adjourn, adjourn, rise to question of privilege, and call for the orders of the day. You can see that if there has been a motion to adjourn, it's more important than the motion a group has been debating (especially if there is some emergency reason to adjourn!). (Privileged motions will be discussed in detail in Chapter 8.)

Incidental motions do not deal with the main motion but instead are concerned with points of order— a member notices something is not happening as it should be or raises a parliamentary question. Someone might make a motion to refer the motion to a committee for further study. The member who made the motion could ask that it be withdrawn, and so on. These motions do not deal with the content of the main motion. (More on incidental motions in the Chapter 9.)

A motion to amend, to adjourn, and so on needs to be addressed before the original main motion is voted upon. So just keep in mind that while main motions are very important, these motions take precedence (have higher "rank"). The steps are:

1. The main motion is proposed.
2. It may be amended.
3. It could be referred to a committee for further study.
4. It could be postponed to a specific time or indefinitely.

5. It is then debated according to the rules of the group or organization.
6. There is a call for the previous question (call for the vote).

Shall We Vote?

Once a member makes a motion, and it's placed before the membership by the chair, it's now the "property" of the membership. That is, the membership decides what will happen to it—whether it's seconded, altered, voted down, and so on. The member who made the motion can ask before a vote if he or she may change the wording, but the members do not need to ask permission to alter the motion.

A group or organization can change voting rules on main motions to require more than a majority vote—to even make it two-thirds of those present if it so desires. This might be a good idea if a main motion is particularly controversial and those present want to make certain that it doesn't just pass by a slim majority. Tread carefully, however, as it may be a device used by those in opposition to a main motion who want it to fail and ask for a larger portion vote to pass in order to help it fail.

Want to change the voting rules on main motions? A member must make a motion to suspend the rules and have another member second the motion. If there is a two-thirds vote to the affirmative, the rule has been changed for the vote on *that* main motion. If, however, the negative votes win, the rules are not changed and there is not a two-thirds vote required to pass the main motion.

 QUESTION?

What if a member enters the meeting during voting?
The proper procedure is to proceed with the vote as if there had been no interruption. The meeting should not be held up so that the latest motion can be explained in order that the member can vote.

The only way that a main motion can be brought up again at the same meeting in which it has been defeated is by having a member who voted on the prevailing side ask that the vote be reconsidered (more on voting in Chapter 13).

Main Motion Pointers

There may seem to be a lot to remember about main motions. The following list might help you to remember the high points:

- Only one main motion can be made at a time. Other motions—such as a motion to amend—can be on the floor, but not two main motions at a time.

Only motions that further the action of considering a main motion can be considered (amend, reconsider, postpone, etc.).

- Phrase your motion in the positive: say, "I move we approve . . ." instead of saying, "I move that we be opposed to" to save confusion.
- It's a good idea to submit your motion or resolution in writing if it's long or complex. Having photocopies of it on hand at the meeting is helpful, too.
- The member who makes the motion is allowed to modify his motion before it's stated by the chair, and can offer an amendment after the chair states it as well.
- Main motions can't change something that has already been adopted, such as the bylaws or special rules of order. There should be language in your bylaws or special rules of order to say when and how these can be changed.
- There's no such action as "tabling a motion." You can't dispose of a motion this way. If you want to postpone it, then word the motion to say that, "I move to postpone the motion to [insert time]."
- New business doesn't always need to be introduced as main motions. "General consent" can be used to save time in some cases.
- Main motions require a second unless they are made by a committee.
- If a main motion seems like a really bad idea, a member can propose that it be "postponed indefinitely."
- Main motions can arise out of a communication

such as a letter or a memo being presented at a meeting.

- Main motions can be in the form of a resolution supporting or opposing a matter.
- The member who makes the motion gets to be the first to speak about it during debate.
- A member has the right to withdraw her main motion up to the time that it's stated by the chair; after that, withdrawal of the motion requires permission from the group or organization.
- To bring the debate on a main motion to a vote, a member should make a motion to "vote on the previous question."
- A main motion may be proposed just once during a meeting. It can be brought up again at another meeting.

The information on main motions in this chapter should serve you well in most situations you will encounter in a group or organization, whether you are leading it or are presenting a main motion. At first, you might want to keep a copy of the most common motions (found in Appendix B of this book) with you for handy reference during a meeting. Soon you'll find that you don't need the list as you gain the confidence found in *doing,* not just thinking about, by leading a meeting or presenting an important matter before it!

Chapter 7

Helping the Main Motion

Main motions are used to introduce new business and involve matters important to the membership. One main motion can sometimes take up an entire meeting. It's vital to know about subsidiary motions that will help a main motion succeed—or fail, if it's not a good idea. Whether you're chairing the meeting or proposing the motion, this chapter will help you know the proper procedure to aid the main motion process.

Amending the Main Motion

An important subsidiary motion is the motion to amend. This is used when a member makes a main motion and others feel that the wording isn't quite right and want to change it. Another member can make a motion to amend the wording before the motion goes to debate.

 ESSENTIAL

> The ability to amend doesn't just belong to other members. The maker of a motion can also amend his own motion. The maker is entitled to amend a motion before the chair states it, but after that, the membership has to agree to any changes.

The motion to amend is the most often used subsidiary motion. Many parliamentarians call it the most important of all the subsidiary motions. Amending a motion can help make it clearer or give it a broader (or more focused) scope. It can also make it into something more likely to be voted for by eliminating some troublesome language before it goes to a vote.

However, the motion to amend can cause a lot of misunderstanding and confusion in a meeting. Some of this can occur simply because a main motion concerns something that is controversial or raises strong emotions within the membership. A motion to spend money can be a touchy issue in any group.

It's often best to have a complex or easily misunderstood motion in writing. This way there can be no doubt of the actual wording of the motion. Then, too, if people feel they must change the motion, they have something to write on (you decide if this is good or bad!).

 FACT

> If a member wants to make an amendment to a motion on the floor, it must be germane to the motion—it must be something that relates to the motion. This prevents the introduction of something that is not concerned with the motion.

Triple Threat

A motion to amend can be done three ways. The first way is with the addition of words or phrases. The second way is to remove words or phrases. The third way is to combine the first two—to add some words and phrases and remove some words and phrases *and* to substitute a paragraph or even a new motion.

Let's say a member makes a motion: "I move that we erect a memorial to veterans of foreign wars in the town square." An example of amending a main motion by inserting a word or phrase might be the following: Another member makes a motion to amend the main motion by inserting the phrase, "with the names of all local veterans inscribed on a marble plaque on the memorial." An example of removing words and phrases is if a member objects to the phrase "foreign wars" and wants to include all veterans, whether they served overseas or in this country.

Finally, an example of the third category (adding and/or removing words or phrases and substituting a paragraph or even a new motion) might be for a member to ask to amend the main motion by making a motion to substitute the new motion: "I move to amend the motion by substituting, "that we hire a consultant to draw up a proposal with estimates of what it will cost to erect a veteran's memorial in the town square." Notice what the last example does: it requires a proposal with costs to be submitted, which is different from the original main motion that would have committed the group or organization to erecting a memorial without any mention of what it might cost—not a good idea at all!

Substituting a motion for another does not mean that it's been adopted. It simply means that it takes the place of that original main motion.

 ALERT!

Tread carefully now! When a member makes a motion to amend by substitution, the chair should point out that a return must be made to the original motion for any further amendments. Then the substitute motion can be discussed and amended. Finally, there's a vote on whether to substitute or not.

Adopting an Amendment

If the membership decides to adopt an amendment, it doesn't mean that things are over. It simply means that the motion on the floor has been changed—and it can be changed again! If the membership votes against the amendment, the original motion stays in its original wording.

If, however, the membership is in favor of the amendment, it is amended. A caution here: this doesn't mean that the motion is adopted—it still hasn't been debated and voted on.

Now, what if another member proposes another amendment? To avoid confusion, the first amendment is referred to as a primary amendment and the amendment to the amendment is considered a secondary amendment.

 FACT

Amendments to motions must be seconded, they are debatable if they are amending a debatable motion, and they require a majority vote even if they are amending a motion that normally requires a two-thirds vote.

If your group has finished amending and discussing, it's time for a vote on the amendments. Votes should be taken in this order: First, the secondary amendment (the amendment to the amendment) should be voted on. Then the primary amendment (the original amendment) is the next to be voted on. Then—finally!—the main motion is voted on. (It's possible that the main motion was amended before a primary and secondary amendment were voted on. Yes, this can be an involved process!)

Amendments: The Good, the Bad, the Ugly

You probably already see the problems inherent in the subsidiary motion of a motion to amend. You're imagining the confusion that can arise from amendments to amendments. Then there's all the time this is taking. The clock is ticking and you're wondering how long this is going to go on. Can't things ever be done the quick and easy way?

Well, no. Sometimes they can't.

Why Amendments Matter

If your group is amending and amending, it means that this matter is something that is very important; it probably can't and shouldn't be rushed, as much as you and others might like it to be. Its importance, too, means there are probably strong emotions involved, and these are getting stirred up. (Imagine the stir that would arise in the example above with the motion to erect a veteran's memorial on the floor!)

Finally, an amendment can be changed so much that its original maker doesn't feel that it is the motion that he or she made to begin with. And it's likely that it isn't;

a member can even make a hostile amendment, one that changes the amendment so much that it doesn't even resemble the original motion—maybe even tries to turn it inside out so it is the opposite of the original.

Here's one important rule to remember—if you're the maker of the original motion *or* if you seconded it, you no longer have the right to amend the motion. Now all you can do is vote against it if it truly is so different that you can't be in favor of it.

The Good News

You're probably wondering if there's anything good about so much amending. Well, yes, there are many good reasons to amend motions. First, the fact that other members are interested enough in your motion to even say anything is positive. Offering suggestions can help improve the motion. As a matter of fact, such motions to amend are called "friendly amendments." Think how ill advised it was for the maker of the motion mentioned earlier to want the motion to erect a memorial passed without specifying a cost.

Is it possible to see that an amendment to your motion is going to help it do what you'd intended more efficiently? There are bad amendments, certainly, which do nothing but thwart what you're trying to do, or seem completely ridiculous. On the other hand, compromise is the name of the game in getting motions passed.

Being willing to compromise over your main motions will go a long way toward showing that you are mature and a good member of your group. This isn't to suggest that you should become a doormat. But think about the character you display when you do not act like a prima donna with regard to your motion, and show that you can work with, not against, other members toward the aim of your group.

 QUESTION?

Too many motions going at one time?
While your group is making motions to amend, some members may be concerned that there is more than one motion on the floor. It's okay—there can be more than one motion while motions to amend are being made.

To Commit or Refer

Committing or referring a motion are subsidiary motions that send it to a committee for further study. The committee can then discuss it and decide what to do with it (such as bring a motion regarding what it thinks should be done). If there is not already a committee set up for study on a similar matter, the group should form one and give it the assignment to study a particular main motion.

But a motion to commit or refer to committee is not specific enough. The motion needs to say to which committee the matter is being referred; if there isn't one already in place and this is a special or ad hoc committee, it will be necessary to state how many members shall serve on the committee, if the membership or the presiding officer shall name its members, and at what future meeting it will report back on its findings.

 ALERT!

> Make certain that when a main motion is referred to a committee, the committee members understand they are to consider not only the motion but any amendments to it that are pending.

This motion needs to be seconded. The only thing that can be debated is whether it should go to a committee (not the content of the motion going to the committee). A majority vote is necessary to pass it. (Remember, when the committee reports to the membership, it does not require a second when it makes a main motion.)

Postponing a Motion

You knew it had to happen. The mayor of your city was scheduled to speak at your meeting and something happened and she didn't arrive on time. So your group went on with its meeting and was in the middle of a main motion when, suddenly, Her Honor appeared at the door, ready to speak. Now what?

It's simple. Postpone the motion until later in the meeting—or even to the next meeting.

There are other good reasons to postpone a group or organization's business: Everything's not in place for a vote, or more information is needed on a motion, or maybe everyone's ready for a recess or wants to call it a night because it's getting late. You'll want to use the subsidiary motion to postpone.

You can use the motion to postpone for all main motions but you must have a member second the motion and get a majority vote to postpone. Debate on the motion of postponing is allowed, but only about whether it's a good idea to postpone; the debate can't go into the main motion that the membership had been discussing. Also, the motion that your group wants to postpone can't be postponed beyond the next meeting or the end of a session or convention.

 ESSENTIAL

> Does a motion look like a really bad idea? Then you might want to use the subsidiary motion to "postpone indefinitely." This will effectively get rid of a motion forever.

If you postpone a motion to a later time and specify that time, then the motion comes up automatically when the time arrives. The motion should be scheduled by your group's presiding officer under unfinished business on the next meeting agenda.

To Limit or End Debate

The subsidiary motion to limit or end debate has saved many a meeting. It's all well and good to have democratic debate in the spirit of Robert's Rules, but if you've ever felt like you're about to scream, "Enough!" in a debate in a meeting, you'll want to know about the subsidiary motion to limit or end debate.

Getting out of Hand?

Some groups specify the rules for debate up front in their bylaws so things don't get out of hand. Sometimes it's because they have large memberships and there's no way that every member can be heard about every specific in every meeting. Sometimes it's because they know there are some people (you know the type!) who will go on and on and on. They could end up monopolizing a debate and that's definitely not to be allowed. Other times, there's going to be a lot of other business to take care of, or you're discussing a particularly controversial issue that isn't likely to be resolved easily. Regulating debate then becomes a good idea.

Start out Right

Right from the start, it's best to set out the terms for debate. The debate rules can be amended but only concerning how long the speeches are and the time that the vote will take place. How much time do you want to allow before a vote? How many members do you have? You might limit debate to two minutes or ten—whatever seems like a good idea for your group.

A member can make a motion such as, "I move that debate on the increase in association dues be limited to one speech of three minutes for each member here tonight." At the end of the scheduled time, the speaker must stop and the next member gets her turn. There is to be no interruption of a speaker or debating what is being said by a speaker—and definitely no disrespect shown.

 QUESTION?

Who keeps track of the time in debates?
The timekeeper does! A motion needs to be made to appoint a member to serve as time-keeper. Whatever method is used to keep time—a clock or a timer—it may still be necessary to tell a speaker that his time is up.

The Previous Question

After everyone has had his or her turn, it's time for a member to make a motion to close debate. An example of this motion is, "I move that the debate be closed and the question of the increase in association dues be put to a vote." Or a more formal way to do this is for a member to say, "I move the previous question." It might seem like a slightly strange thing to say the first time you say it, but it's correct.

Be careful before using the subsidiary motion to close debate. Have you paid attention to the rules of the debate? Has the pending motion been debated? Have all the scheduled speakers spoken and the time for the debate run out? Only then should you make this motion, or the presiding officer will rule you out of order.

Does one call the question require second debate?

 ALERT!

Sometimes a member who has been attending meetings for a long time might try to save time by just calling out, "Question!" Don't do this, as it's considered rude.

There is, by the way, no debating the motion to end debate. It requires a second, and two-thirds of the members must be in favor of closing the debate.

As you can see, main motions just couldn't exist without subsidiary motions. Motions to amend, to postpone, to refer to committees, to limit or extend debate, to move the previous question to proceed to a vote . . . it might seem like a lot to remember, but it's not. Just imagine that each is a block needed to build a successful main motion. All members can serve their group or organization better by understanding these subsidiary motions and using them correctly.

Chapter 8

It's a Question of Privilege

Privileged motions are just that—they address privileges. Whose privileges? The privileges of the most important people to any group or organization: its members and the group or organization itself. General privilege is the privileged motion that concerns the organization; personal privilege is the form of privileged motion that concerns its individuals. Should the membership take a recess? Is there some reason to adjourn early? A privileged motion can interrupt business to take care of these situations.

"Privileged" Defined

A privileged motion is the highest-ranking motion because it interrupts business to take care of urgent issues. It calls a halt to what is going on in a meeting to take a recess or to adjourn or to raise a question. When a privileged motion is made, it doesn't have anything to do with any motion that's pending. If there's a motion on the floor to consider an issue, the privileged motion won't have anything to do with the content of that pending motion. But you *will* be interrupting what's being considered to raise your privileged motion.

The Privileged Motions

This chapter gives you an overview of the motions, from the highest ranked (most important) to the lowest ranked (least important). However, what really makes a motion important and valuable to you is what goal you use it to achieve—to adjourn early if there's a need, to ask for a recess in a long and stressful meeting, or to speak up in an urgent situation.

The motions, from highest ranked to lowest ranked, are:

1. Fix the time *to* which to adjourn/Fix the time *at* which to adjourn
2. Adjourn
3. Recess
4. Question of privilege
5. Call for orders of the day

Tap into the Power

It's important to remember that meetings run by Robert's Rules are run democratically. When meetings are run without regard to the comfort of all members, go for long periods of time without a break, or ignore the times set for votes and other important matters, members are likely to feel that they and their needs are not being taken seriously. Becoming familiar with privileged motions and using them to be fair and courteous while conducting group or organization business will go a long way toward making members feel privileged to be a part of it!

Fix the Time *to* Which to Adjourn

The language of this motion can be confusing. You hear the phrase "an adjourned meeting" and you think it's one that's adjourned—members have gone home. But, in fact, it means that a meeting is adjourned to another time. The motion sets another, later date to continue the meeting before a regular meeting.

Perhaps there is too much business to transact in a regular or special meeting and the group or organization needs another one before its next regular meeting to take care of this. The current meeting isn't adjourned when members leave—the meeting is continued into another meeting. Its time and date are stated within the motion.

There are positives and negatives to the fix the time *to* which to adjourn privileged motion. Another meeting gives members a chance to finish business that is taking more time than they expected. It means that members don't become overtired or irritable, as they do when meetings go into overtime.

FACT

This motion could be considered an incidental main motion (more on incidental motions in Chapter 9) if it's made when no business is pending, which means that it could be open to debate. If you don't want to have a debate, make the motion when business is pending.

One negative is that people lead busy lives these days, and they may not be happy if they have to return for another meeting. Another negative is that setting up meetings outside the regular times and dates can also confuse people, especially if they miss a meeting at which the new meeting is announced and hear about it from someone who attended.

To make the motion to fix the time *to* which to adjourn, a member should say: "I move that when this meeting adjourns today, it adjourns to meet [on this day] at [this time]." Another member will need to second the motion. This motion is not open to debate but can be reconsidered. It must have a majority vote to adopt.

Fix the Time *at* Which to Adjourn

Here's the perfect motion for members who don't want a meeting to drag on and on. It sets the time for adjournment ahead of time. The membership must adjourn at the preset time. The chair is responsible for announcing that the time has come for adjournment, and then she should adjourn the meeting.

There are obvious benefits to having a prearranged time to adjourn. Members don't worry that business will be conducted past a certain time. There's nothing worse than waiting for a certain matter to come up so you can have your say about it, only to have to leave and find out later that it came up after you left.

Preserving a Quorum

It may be easier for your group or organization to preserve a quorum if members know that a meeting will definitely be over at a certain time. Giving notice of the time the meeting will adjourn makes it possible for members to make plans accordingly. Then, too, members don't feel that they are being held hostage by a group that wants to keep everyone talking about a matter until the wee hours.

Making the Motion

To make a motion to fix the time *at* which to adjourn, a member should say, "I move that the meeting adjourn at [time]." Another member needs to make a motion to second, and because this motion is made when no business is pending, it's an incidental main motion and debate can take place. A majority is needed to adopt and the motion can't be reconsidered.

QUESTION?

Does this mean we *have* to stay until the set time?
No. A motion to fix the time *at* which to adjourn simply sets the time to adjourn, but if the membership wants to adjourn *before* that time, that's okay. A member should make the usual motion to adjourn.

Can We Go Home Now? (Adjourn)

Is your meeting running overtime for some reason? Have you become aware of an impending severe thunderstorm and you're concerned about the safety of members who have to drive home in it? Or maybe the power suddenly goes out. This might be a good time to adjourn.

The Motion to Adjourn

The procedure to make the motion is the same as it is with the motion to recess. You shouldn't interrupt another speaker unless there is an urgent need to do so (such as the power suddenly going out). Again, gain the attention of the chair and say, "I move that we adjourn as the hour is late."

The motion must be seconded, but unlike the motion to recess, the motion to adjourn cannot be debated or amended. An important point must be stressed here: You need to know whether the rules for your group or organization allow for another meeting if you need to adjourn before the business is finished. If so, then you can make a motion to adjourn while there is business pending. Remember, the motion must be seconded and a majority vote is required. The motion can't be reconsidered, but if it's not approved, it can be made again later in the meeting.

Wait a Minute!

There are times when it's not appropriate to adjourn. One of these times is when a group or organization is in the midst of voting. If a motion to adjourn is made before voting is completed or verified, the chair should explain that this is not correct. The only exception is if a vote has been made by ballot. As long as all the ballots have been collected, the meeting may be adjourned and those in charge of counting the ballots may continue to do their work.

 ESSENTIAL

> After a vote to adjourn is adopted, members can still make motions to reconsider a vote or reconsider a vote and enter on the minutes if they do so *before* the chair adjourns the meeting.

If a member has made a motion to adjourn, the chair needs to tie up any loose ends that may exist. If there is business that needs to be taken care of, announcements that need to be made, motions to reconsider the vote on a previous motion or to reconsider the vote and enter on the minutes, the chair should inform the membership of these.

Lunch—Please? (Recess)

Has the midday meeting gone on for so long that people look ready to faint from hunger? It might be time to make a motion for a recess—a break or suspension in the meeting. After all, not only is it hard to concentrate when you're hungry, but it might be difficult to hear if there's a lot of stomach rumbling from hunger pangs! People find it difficult to be interested in business when they need to address their personal needs.

Perhaps instead of taking a lunch break, your group or organization needs a stress break. If a controversial issue has divided your membership into two opposing factions and nerves are fraying in debate, a recess might be just what's needed. Taking a short—or long!—break can help members retreat to neutral corners and, afterward, approach the issue in a more conciliatory manner. If things are still heated after the break, well, at least everyone got a little time away!

Save Your Sanity—and Your Group

The privileged motion to take a recess is one that has saved more than one group or organization from splintering. Sometimes the only way to get some perspective is to get out of a meeting room and away from hearing—and thinking—about an issue. If someone on "the other side" of the issue is using persistence and a loud voice to hammer home a point, it might be a little hard to convince him that a recess is a good idea, but chances are, other members may be in agreement with you.

The Motion for Recess

To make a motion for a recess, you should first make certain that you are not interrupting any speaker. Gain the attention of the chair and say, "The time is [time]. I move that we recess for lunch and return at [new time]." Another member must second the motion. Other members can debate the amount of time for the recess and amend it, but not the motion to recess itself. Of course, the usual rules about amending motions apply here: There's a vote on whether there is approval of the amendment. The membership votes on the motion to recess and there must be a majority (not a two-thirds) vote.

 ALERT!

Choose the length of your recess carefully. If it's too short, members may come back late. Too long a recess, and members could be tempted to just leave and not come back.

It's Hot, It's Cold, It's Confidential (Question)

There are two forms of question of privilege motions: general and personal. General is used for matters that relate to the group or organization as a whole. It is used when there's a really urgent reason to interrupt the proceedings. Perhaps the room is so uncomfortably warm that members feel they just can't sit through another minute of the meeting unless the temperature is lowered. Or, the opposite: Members are turning into icicles because either the air-conditioning has made the room frigid or it's winter and there's no heat.

Perhaps members can't hear the proceedings because the microphone isn't working. Or perhaps they're hearing a little too much: Something confidential is brought up and a member realizes that there is a guest present and the chair isn't responding to this.

It's time to act! A member should stand and address the chair, saying, "I rise to a question of privilege that affects the assembly." The chair should ask the member to state the question of privilege. Here is where the member should state the problem quickly and suggest a remedy: "The room is too hot. Could the thermostat be turned down, please?"

Do We Need a Motion?

It's possible that the situation is serious and requires a motion, especially if it's a matter of confidentiality, mentioned above. The chair can ask that the question be put into the form of a motion; if he doesn't, a member should say, "I move that we excuse our guest and go into executive session to discuss this confidential matter." Another member should second this motion and then there will be the usual debate and vote just as there is with other motions.

 ESSENTIAL

> Sometimes it's necessary to interrupt business with an urgent motion of privilege. The chair rules on whether it should interrupt business. There is no debate or amending. However, if no business is pending, the motion may be debated and amended.

Hey, It's Personal!

The personal privilege affects individual members, not the entire group or organization. Did someone misquote you? When minutes of a previous meeting were read, did you, for example, notice that there was a mistake in the record of who attended? Was there a mention of something relating to an individual member that is incorrect?

It's time to raise a question of privilege by using the same method as was used above for the general privilege: Stand; address the chair; say, "I rise to a question of personal privilege"; and state what the problem is. As with other motions, there must be a second, debate, and vote.

Speaking Up

Do you object to the way you're being portrayed by a speaker? Perhaps in a debate a member makes a remark that is not true or misquotes something another said. The member who feels that he has been mis-quoted or misstated should make a motion of personal privilege.

Hey, I Didn't Say That!

If you're the member who feels maligned by a speaker, and the chair hasn't spoken up, you don't have to stay silent about it. Wait until the speaker is finished—unless the offense is too great—and gain the attention of the chair. If you've been misquoted, you might say, "The speaker is misquoting my remarks."

Remember that this is not the time to duplicate the behavior you're protesting. Keep to a higher standard, and keep your cool. Don't launch a tirade or start a speech. Simply correct the misquote and be seated.

Back to Work

After the question of privilege has been taken care of, the business that was on the floor resumes. It isn't necessary to make a motion to ask that this be done. The previous business should simply be taken up again. The speaker whose remarks were interrupted with a question of privilege is to be given the floor again. Back to work!

FACT

The membership doesn't always have to take action on a question of privilege when it is raised. It can also be referred to a committee or be "laid on the table" (deferred to a future time for study).

Call for Orders of the Day

It might seem like a strange term, this *call for orders of the day*. You might be thinking you're going to be subjected to some regimented, military-style routine, and while Robert *was* an Army man, this isn't what the term means.

An agenda or order of business is used to conduct business at a meeting. Both of these items help the membership to use an ordered outline of the business topics that will be discussed and acted upon. There may be special times set for discussion of certain motions or for voting.

Getting Sidetracked

Even the best-run meetings (and the best people running them) can get sidetracked or start to run long. Members start checking their watches, looking concerned. After all, it's 9 A.M. and the vote on buying that new equipment was scheduled for 8:30. Everyone has a busy day ahead of them and there's longwinded Mr.

Sanders going on and on and no one seems willing to do anything. After all, he's the boss's brother . . . but at this rate, it'll be lunchtime before anyone gets back to the office.

Time to Make the Call

This is the perfect time to use this privileged motion. All it takes is one member who will rise and call for the orders of the day—a request that the matter that was scheduled be conducted. It's the right thing to do. After all, there was a reason for setting a time for whatever the matter is to be discussed and acted on, and members may have come to the meeting for that reason alone. They shouldn't have to leave because it's looking like it's not going to be brought up. If they do leave, your quorum may go with them.

The Motion for the Call

If you've got a longwinded speaker, you'll need to be courteous to make your motion. Avoid the temptation to interrupt; hopefully, you have an observant chair who may be on the verge of moving things along. Rise and wait to be recognized, and then say, "I call for the orders of the day."

This motion does not require a second. It can't be amended or debated. Now the chair must immediately proceed with the orders of the day.

If, however, the chair or a member feels it would be better to stay with the current discussion, then a vote should be taken to "set aside" the orders of the day.

A two-thirds vote (not a simple majority) decides whether the orders should be set aside (so the current discussion can go on) *or* the membership should proceed with the orders of the day. Chances are, if the order of the day was important enough to set a time to do it, the membership will want to take care of it.

 QUESTION?

> **Remember the Three Musketeers' vow?**
> It was "all for one and one for all." One member can call for the orders of the day for the good of all members. He or she can ask that the meeting proceed to the orders. No second is necessary.

When All Else Fails

All of us have probably been around people who just want to push through 'til the bitter end. You know, the type of member who says, "We're already here, we've talked about this a lot. I'm willing to stay until it's resolved." Maybe we've even been those people. And yes, there's a lot to be said for staying with something to get it resolved rather than having to deal with it over and over.

But maybe you just can't sit through a six-hour meeting on top of your workday (and you only had time for a crummy sandwich all day). Or, you've had to attend a second meeting because the first was adjourned to another time to continue what should have been settled at the first meeting. You care passionately about this group or organization but you just can't bear another minute in this hard chair discussing something that should have been settled ages ago.

Keep a Cool Head

If you're the chair, keep in mind that there are very real reasons why members can't stay at a meeting indefinitely or attend second, even third, meetings to finish business. Keep an eye out for potential problems. The longer a meeting goes—especially if it's an evening meeting—or the more the business is extended to other meetings, the more tired members become. They may be less than cooperative and reasonable conducting business.

Be prepared to be an arbiter if one group wants to be the type to push, push, push to get through and another group wants to call it a day. Remember, if the group who wants to leave does so, it might eliminate your quorum, which means everything's over for that meeting anyway.

Knowing When to Quit

If you're a member and there have been motions to adjourn that have failed and your chair seems to be one of those stick-to-it types, there's not a lot you can do. Leave if you must (quietly, of course), and don't feel you're obligated to make excuses as to why. Even the most like-minded group can have different opinions about things, but there should be no arguing over who is more committed to the group simply because one side wants to stay longer than the other over a matter.

 ALERT!

> As members begin to leave a long or late-hour meeting, keep an eye on your quorum requirements, or you may find that your group or organization is conducting business that won't be official.

If you've ever sat in a meeting room that was too hot or so cold that your teeth were chattering and you thought you had to put up with it, now you know differently. You have the information you need to bring up the situation in the proper way. Stuck in a meeting that's going nowhere fast and you need to get home or get back to the office? Reach into this chapter for the motions to adjourn or fix the time to adjourn or—well, you get the message. Knowing about privileged motions and using them correctly in your meetings will help you accomplish more (and enjoy more) whether you are a chair or a member.

Chapter 9

Not So Incidental

Incidental motions are concerned with enforcing correct procedures as your group or organization deals with a main motion in a meeting. Incidental motions will help you raise a point of order (a breach of the rules), appeal a decision of the chair, make requests and ask questions, and do many other important things related to main motions. Though they are called "incidental," there's nothing incidental about their role in the pending business of your group or organization.

Types of Incidental Motions

One definition of the word *incidental* is "minor or subordinate," but there's nothing minor or subordinate about the effect of an incidental motion. The other definition of *incidental* is "occurring at the same time or as a result." That's what incidental motions really do—they occur at the same time or as a result of a main motion.

Incidental motions are equal—there is no incidental motion more important or less important than another. The following is a list of the types of incidental motions you may encounter:

Point of order
Appeal
Division of the assembly
Request for permission to withdraw/modify a motion
Objection to consideration of a question
Request to be excused from a duty
Requests and inquiries
Division of the question
Suspend the rules

As you can see, all of the above incidental motions are very important. A meeting couldn't be conducted without them. An incidental motion is powerful when you consider that there must be action on it before the business of the meeting continues.

When should you make an incidental motion? That's easy—right away, while the main motion is being considered. Perhaps you see a problem with the main motion. You might want to withdraw it or modify it. Don't wait for objections to it. Act and take care of it before the matter goes to debate and then a vote. Do you feel the chair ruled incorrectly? Make an appeal.

 ESSENTIAL

> Incidental motions are different from subsidiary motions in that they don't relate to the main motion during the full time that it is on the floor. An incidental motion is made to make certain that the correct procedure is taking place while a main motion is considered.

Point of Order

Has a member done something incorrect in a meeting? Has the chair? Perhaps a vote has just been taken on a main motion but you realize that there is no longer a quorum. This is something that takes place frequently during a meeting. Often the chair is so occupied with keeping a debate on track—especially if there is controversy and strong emotion during the meeting—that she has not noticed the problem of the lack of a quorum.

Or perhaps debate begins on a main motion but no one seconded the motion. This might seem like a small thing, but it isn't. Sometimes a member makes a motion because he thinks it's important, but no one else does, so no debate is necessary. Why waste the time of the membership?

Raising a Point of Order

The procedure of raising a point of order is a simple one. All that's necessary is for a member to say, "I rise to a point of order." The chair will ask what the point is and a member should state what it is; for example, "There was no second on the motion so debate should not proceed." Or, if there is no longer a quorum, then the member should state, "We no longer have a quorum so any business that is transacted is null and void."

Important Things to Remember

Always be sure of your facts before you rise to a point of order. Since you've taken the time to read this guide, you will have a good understanding of Robert's Rules. Take care not to personally malign any member as you make the motion—a motion to appeal should be strictly on procedure. The chair may or may not rule the way you want. (Read on to see how to appeal a decision of the chair.)

 ALERT!

Remember that incidental motions take precedence over all motions except for privileged motions. What you are raising in an incidental motion is an immediate procedural point that is to be addressed right away.

Appeal

Raising an appeal means that a member's disagreement with the chair's decision on any motion on the floor becomes a matter for the membership to decide. An appeal should never be proposed for trivial, frivolous, or malicious reasons, because this could diminish its effect when raised at other times—kind of like crying wolf.

However, appealing the chair's decision on a matter is a wonderful checks-and-balances feature of parliamentary procedure. It can prevent an abuse of the power that the position of chair holds. An additional check is that another member must second the motion to appeal. This way, if there is a member who is always disgruntled with what's going on at a meeting, he alone cannot prevent any business from being accomplished.

The Appeal Motion

To appeal the decision of the chair, a motion must be made immediately, not later on in the meeting as an afterthought. The chair gets first right to speak after the motion is made and the motion is debatable unless it's about a rule of speaking, a ruling on a motion that was not debatable, or the order of business. The motion isn't amendable but it can be reconsidered.

To make an appeal, a member should say, "I appeal the decision of the chair." If another member seconds the motion, the chair may speak about why he made the decision (ruling). The maker of the motion to appeal should listen carefully to the explanation because it may be that it makes sense and the motion should be withdrawn. Other members may also speak once.

 ESSENTIAL

> Has a member asked the chair a parliamentary question? Perhaps a member wants to know if it's correct to make a motion. An appeal can't be made to the chair because she has given an opinion, not a decision. The member can still make the motion.

Now What?

After everyone who wants to speak has done so, the chair gets another opportunity, and then a vote should be taken. The chair should say, "The question is, shall the decision of the chair be sustained? All who are in favor say 'aye.' Those opposed should say 'no.'" Then the chair announces the vote. A majority (not two-thirds) is necessary for the decision to be sustained. If the chair's decision is sustained, the chair will say, "The ayes have it and the decision of the chair is sustained." If the vote is in the negative, the chair should say, "The no's have it and the decision of the chair is reversed."

Division of the Assembly

Something smell fishy? Has a vote has been taken and you don't think that the results are correct? If the vote has been done by ballot, you wonder if some votes have been computed in error. Or perhaps the vote was so close that you feel that it would be a good idea to contest the matter. Make a motion for division.

This is not a time to dawdle. If you have any question about the results of a vote, you must make a motion now. The chair announces the result and it stands if there is no protest. Other business of the meeting may be affected by this vote, so it's important to make certain that all is correct.

This motion is very important because it concerns the procedure of voting. It's so important that it does *not* require a second, and there can be no debate. A member feels the voting has been incorrectly or inappropriately carried out and makes a motion? That's it; the voting procedure is addressed. End of story.

 FACT

Doubts about the results of ballot votes or roll call votes can be alleviated by making a motion to recount. This motion will require a majority vote unless your group's or organization's rules state otherwise.

To propose the motion, a member should simply say, "Division" or "I doubt [or question] the results of the vote." The chair must then retake the vote using a different method than was used the first time. Was the vote taken by voice vote? It should be retaken another way, perhaps by a standing vote.

If there is still doubt about the vote—and there can be if the vote is being taken in a large room, for instance, and members shift around while the vote is being taken—the chair takes the vote again, perhaps by having members count off. The secretary should record the exact vote (the numbers of affirmative and negative votes) in the minutes. (Read more about voting and its inherent problems in Chapter 13.)

Request for Permission to Withdraw/Modify a Motion

These motions are used frequently. A member might have risen to make a motion and realized that he misjudged the timing or the mood of the membership on the issue the motion concerned. Making a motion to modify or even withdraw the main motion might be a very wise move. The maker of a motion "owns" it before the chair states it. If you're thinking of withdrawing your motion, do it before the chair has a chance to state it. You can even withdraw your motion if another member has seconded it. To withdraw a motion, a member needs to simply say, "I ask permission to withdraw the motion."

However, after the motion has been stated by the chair, the motion is owned by the assembly. If the maker of the motion wants to withdraw it, he must get the permission of the assembly to do so. The chair can simplify this by using unanimous consent; that is, she can say, "If there is no objection, the motion is withdrawn." The person who seconded it does not have a say in whether the motion is withdrawn. The group or organization secretary does not record a withdrawn motion in the minutes.

Modifying the Motion

Have you made a motion and suddenly realized that you need to modify it? Perhaps you realized that your wording isn't quite as clear as you'd originally thought it was, or that you should add a dollar amount or a date or other detail. Again, a member owns the motion until the chair states it. So, if you want to modify your motion, do it immediately. Say, "I wish to modify my motion by [adding such-and-such]." If the original motion was seconded but the modification is not something that member now agrees with, he can withdraw his second.

 ESSENTIAL

> Any member has an opportunity to ask the maker of a motion if he will accept a modification before the chair states the motion. If the maker rejects it, the member can still try to make a change by making a motion to amend after it's stated by the chair.

The chair will then state the new, modified motion. If a member seconded it and withdrew his support, then another member will need to second the motion. After that, there is the usual debate, then a vote.

Objection to Consideration of a Question

Uh-oh. Here it comes. You-know-who is going to spoil a perfectly lovely meeting by getting up to propose *that* motion. You know the one. There's one in every group, it seems. Someone with a pet motion to fund a pet project and it's set to divide the group straight down the middle. You can almost feel members getting ready to pop an antacid.

The objection to consideration of a question is perfect for this situation. Any member can propose it and it doesn't need a second, isn't debatable, and isn't amendable. A vote on it is taken even before any discussion (by that longwinded member—isn't it always a longwinded member who gets these ideas?). Perfect, right?

How It Works

This motion is designed to prevent the consideration—the discussion and acting upon—of a main motion (question). It's like holding up a hand to stop someone from talking. The motion should be used carefully. Used too often, it could become rude and obstructive. But used carefully, sparingly, it might be your best tool for keeping one member or one issue from dividing the group and making a meeting unpleasant or needlessly focused on an issue no one wants to hear about.

Give Me the Tool

To stop the consideration of a question (motion), a member should say, "I object to consideration of the question." That's it. Couldn't be simpler, right? The chair should immediately take a vote by saying, "The consideration of the question is objected to. Shall the question be considered?" A vote should be taken by the method used by the group, whether it's voice or by standing. If two-thirds of those present don't want to consider the question, then it can't be considered for the rest of the meeting.

Unfortunately, you know you-know-who. He or she will probably be back at another meeting to propose it. Some people never learn. But you and your group or organization will have the motion to object to consideration of a question, and maybe eventually you-know-who will get the message!

 ALERT!

Remember, Robert's Rules are concerned with being both democratic and courteous. If you're worried that consideration of a motion will cause division, use democracy and courtesy when you make the motion to prevent consideration or you'll just cause more division!

Request to Be Excused from a Duty

Most people join a group or organization with the best of intentions. They really want to be a part of things, to give of themselves, their talents, and, occasionally, their money. But sometimes, there just isn't enough time in the day for everything we want to do.

Maybe you've been asked to serve on a committee or as an officer and you just can't fulfill your obligations. Maybe the reason you joined the group or organization just isn't there anymore and you want to move on to other interests. Maybe—worst case scenario here—you've been charged with a breach of conduct. Now what?

Please Excuse Me

First, remember that if you are asked to perform a duty, you may decline it if it's not mandatory to belonging to your group or organization. If you're an officer, for example, the secretary, and you don't want to continue to take minutes (which is a mandatory duty for the secretary in your group or organization), then you should be asked to be excused from your office. Resigning is a choice if the group no longer is something you want to be a part of. If you've committed a breach of conduct or you just don't feel it's worth it to fight proceedings against you, then it's wise to resign.

How to Be Excused

If the duty is not mandatory, decline at the time it's offered; it's not necessary to ask the membership for permission. If you can't continue in an office, then you should submit your resignation in writing to the secretary. The resignation will be put to a vote and you can't discontinue performing your duties until the resignation is accepted (if there's an emergency situation, your group or organization may make other arrangements).

If you want to resign, some groups won't let you if your dues are outstanding. If you refuse or can't pay, you chance being expelled (which may have negative connotations you would prefer to avoid). Finally, if you have exhibited bad conduct and are charged with such, your group or organization may be happy to receive your resignation and accept it, although it has the option of refusing and may proceed with your trial.

 ESSENTIAL

Watch out if someone uses the expression "Busy people get things done" as a way to persuade you to take on a duty. Don't let anyone convince you to take on more than you can handle. Who needs the embarrassment of having to ask to be excused from a duty later when it gets to be too much?

Requests, Inquiries, and Other Incidental Motions

Some incidental motions make requests and inquiries. A few of these have already been discussed earlier in this chapter. There are a number of lesser known or used incidental motions that make requests and inquiries.

Parliamentary inquiries are incidental motions. A member might ask for clarification on a point of parliamentary procedure. When the chair answers such an inquiry, the member(s) should understand that the chair is giving an opinion, not a decision.

If a member wants information, he or she can say, "I rise for information" or "I rise to a point of information." Sometimes members want to read a paper (more on this later); it's allowed only if no member objects.

Does your group or organization have bylaws or rules concerning nominations? Most do. However, if the answer is no, then there may be interest in incidental motions relating to these. If there's a pending election, any member can make a motion that sets up the way he or she would like to see nominations made for office. Sometimes members may have many different methods to propose; these can be proposed as amendments to the motion. Time should be allowed for nominations before the chair asks if there are further nominations, then if there aren't, the chair can use general consent to close the nomination process (which eliminates a need to have a member make a motion to close nominations).

Incidental motions relating to nominations must be seconded. They can be amended but are not debatable, and they must have a majority vote (if there's a motion to close nominations, it will require a two-thirds vote in the affirmative). You'll learn more about nominations and voting in Chapters 13 and 14.

Division of the Question (Motion)

Has a question (motion) come on the floor that is so involved you feel that it should be divided up and voted on in separate parts? The longer and more complicated a motion, the better chance that members may not understand it. And if they don't understand it or if parts make them nervous, they may vote down the motion.

The maker of the motion doesn't "own" the motion after the chair has stated it, so you don't need his permission to divide it. Look at the motion and see if it can be broken down into separate motions. If it can, a motion to divide is definitely in order.

 FACT

Want to support just one part of a motion? If a member wants to divide a motion so that just one part of it can be voted upon, she can make a motion to that effect.

A member should say, "I move to divide the motion into [number of] parts. The first motion is to [state the motion]. The second motion is to [state the motion] . . . ," and so on, for as many parts as the motion needs to be divided into. This motion to divide needs to be seconded. It is not debatable. The chair can now put the motion to divide to a vote, or the chair can use general (unanimous) consent and ask the membership, "Is there any objection to dividing the motion into [number of] parts? Hearing none, the motion is divided." If there are objections, the original motion with all its complexities stands.

Suspend the Rules

Is there a reason that your group or organization wants to take up business out of its usual order on the agenda? There may be a reason for discussing new business before old business is addressed. Perhaps it's getting late and there's a general feeling that the membership doesn't want to debate a particular motion and prefers to suspend the rules of the assembly about debate.

Rules That Cannot Be Changed

There are certain things that cannot be changed by a suspension of the rules. Bylaws can't be changed except by special meeting (see Chapter 2). Corporate charters and parliamentary procedure can't be changed. Any rule that protects the rights of individual members, especially members who are absent, can't be set aside by a suspension of rules. A suspension of the rules isn't intended to "sneak in" and change the fabric of integrity in the group or organization. It should be used only for setting aside rules that pertain to normal business.

How to Make the Motion

If a member wants to suspend the rules, she should say, "I move to suspend the rules and take up [another matter]." There must be a second. Then the chair should call for a vote; passage requires a two-thirds majority vote in favor of suspension. Or the chair can use general (unanimous) consent by saying, "Is there any objection to suspending the rules and taking up [the other matter]? Hearing none, the rules are suspended and the next item on the agenda is [new matter]." If there is an objection, there must be a vote.

Incidental motions help enforce correct procedures in your group or organization meeting. Some, like the motion to object to consideration of a question, can save you and others so much time and aggravation. Knowing how to appeal a decision of the chair or how to challenge a vote that doesn't seem correct provides checks and balances to keep things democratic. Aren't you glad you're becoming more knowledgeable about Robert's Rules? (Do we hear a nomination for you as an officer? Hmm?)

Chapter 10

Bringing Back a Motion

Someone wants to bring back that motion that the membership didn't deal with at the time it was originally proposed. Perhaps it wasn't an opportune time. The content of the motion might have been controversial and a member made a motion to push it forward to this meeting. Or maybe there was bad weather that night and people started leaving, and suddenly there was no quorum. For whatever reason, it's time to act on the motion.

Let's Hear It Again!

Bringing a motion before the membership again is called "returning a question to the assembly." Perhaps you feel your motion didn't get a fair chance at a past meeting. Maybe it's a motion that someone else proposed and you'd like to support it.

There are a number of ways to do this. One way is to renew a motion. If a motion has been defeated, it's possible to reintroduce it at the next meeting of the group or organization. (The only time it can be reintroduced at the same meeting is if it's been changed so much that it's essentially a new motion or a different procedure is used.)

 ALERT!

It's vital to remember that when renewing a motion, it can't be changed in any way. It must be the same exact motion that was laid on the table, unchanged. If there have been any changes in wording, it must be proposed as a new motion.

If a motion has been set aside temporarily (laid on the table), members must take it from the table by the end of the next meeting of the group or organization or the motion will die. The process is simple. Any member can make this motion as long as no other business is pending.

To renew a motion, a member should say, "I move to take from the table the motion [to do X]." Another member seconds the motion, and the chair proceeds with the vote. If there's a majority in favor of it, the motion is once again before the membership.

Rescind or Amend Something Previously Adopted

Have you or a member of your group or organization changed your mind about a motion that has been adopted? The motion might have been made with the best of intentions. It might have been discussed by the best minds in the group. Emotion might have ruled the debate, and the vote, that night. Maybe some important information wasn't available at the time. It's time to think about rescinding the motion—or, its companion motion, amend something previously adopted. If action has not been taken on the motion and it is not impossible to change it, you and your group or organization are in luck.

Let's Take Another Look

Did you open the newspaper this morning and find out that there are problems at the place where your group or organization was planning to send a donation? It might be a bad idea to send that donation until you get more information. Perhaps members wanted to start building the clubhouse, but some changes in the membership situation since that vote was taken have caused many of you to question that original decision.

 QUESTION?

What if someone resigns but then changes his mind?
A resignation cannot be rescinded if action has been taken on it and the member notified. Likewise, if a member has been expelled or removed from office and notified, this action can't be rescinded.

Previous Notice

Robert's Rules mandate previous notice if a group or organization wants to rescind or amend something previously adopted. This can be done by notifying the membership in writing by mail or e-mail or fax. Or a member can give verbal notice at the meeting before the one at which he or she will be making the motion. To do this, the member should say, "I rise to give previous notice that at the next meeting I'll be making a motion to rescind the action [to do X]."

If there is no previous notice, then there must be a two-thirds or majority of the membership (not a majority of those present at that meeting) vote for it to be adopted. This is so that the rights of the membership aren't abridged.

Making the Motion

To make a motion to rescind or amend something previously adopted, a member should say, "I move to rescind the action [to do X]." Another member then needs to second the motion. At this point, if previous notice was given, the chair should note this to the membership, tell them that a majority is needed to adopt, and ask if there is any discussion. After any discussion, the group votes.

If, however, there has not been previous notice, the chair should mention this to the membership. At that point, the chair should remind the membership that the motion needs a two-thirds vote to pass (see Appendix B for a list of motions that require two-thirds or a majority vote). If the motion is adopted, the motion that had been adopted previously is reversed. If there is a negative vote, the motion to rescind or amend something previously adopted may be reconsidered later.

 ALERT!

The previous notice requirement was invented for a reason—there may be members who are unhappy that a motion passed who decide to try to rescind it or amend it to their own ends later. With previous notice, members can be alerted to a potential change.

More Amendments

What if you want to amend a motion that's been previously adopted? Perhaps your group has decided to put a plaque honoring the past president of the group on the clubhouse wall. Then someone notices that this has not been done in the past. Maybe it's a really good idea, but all past presidents should be honored.

Get It Right!

To amend the motion mentioned above, a member might say, "I move to amend the motion to place a plaque on the clubhouse wall honoring Mildred Smith, the past president of our group, by striking out 'Mildred Smith' and inserting the names of all past presidents." Then another member should second the motion. The chair should ask if there is any discussion on the proposed amendment. Then a vote is in order. The same vote conditions for passage exist as for rescinding—two-thirds vote or a majority of the entire membership.

Leaving Well Enough Alone

There are some motions previously adopted that cannot be amended. Anything that exceeds the scope of the original motion can't be tampered with. Many groups or organizations also have language in their bylaws to ensure that constitutions, bylaws, and other governing instruments can't be changed from meeting to meeting.

If there is not such language, then these items can be changed with the same voting requirements listed above for rescinding/amending something previously adopted. This can mean there's more chance for constant change that might not be in the best interests of any group or organization. Great thought and sometimes legal advice are used in the writing of constitutions and bylaws; changes made by members who might be uninformed about the original purpose of some language could cause problems if they're done in a regular meeting.

Discharging a Committee

The committee that was appointed to study a main motion . . . hasn't. Or maybe they've met over and over again and they still have failed to do much of anything. If the committee is not a standing committee and was appointed solely to study a main motion, nothing can be done on it until the committee makes a recommendation. Perhaps something has happened that makes taking action on a main motion urgent. Whatever the reason—urgent or otherwise—it has become necessary for the membership to do something. It's also, after all, a very real concern that the main motion could die in committee.

First, Give 'Em a Deadline

Is the date for a meeting when you want to take care of a main motion you've referred to committee coming up? Don't panic. The first thing that a group or organization can do is give a committee a deadline to report (it can even make it a special order so that it comes up at a specific time on the agenda). A motion to set a time to report requires only a majority vote to adopt. A chair or a membership should use foresight and give a committee a date to report by. Sending a motion or a matter to study to a committee is supposed to *save* time, aggravation, and controversy, not *cause* it by not reporting on time!

If the committee still fails to report, the membership can take the matter out of its hands. First, no other business can be ongoing when a motion to discharge the committee takes place. Previous notice should be given, either in written form such as a letter or e-mail or fax, or orally at the meeting before the one where the discharge of committee motion will take place.

Making the Motion

A member wishing to make a motion to discharge a committee should make certain that previous notice has been given, or the chair will have to note the fact before a vote is taken. Without previous notice, either a two-thirds vote or a majority of the entire membership is needed; with previous notice, a majority vote is needed to adopt.

There are two different ways to take a main motion from consideration by a committee. If it is a standing committee, a member should say, "I move that the [X committee] be discharged from further consideration of the motion [X]." If it's a special committee appointed to study a certain motion or matter, then a member should say, "I move to discharge the committee to which was referred the motion relating to [X]."

 FACT

> If the committee is a standing committee, it remains in effect. If the committee is a special one, appointed to study a particular motion or matter, then it goes out of existence forever when the membership vote discharges the committee.

Both motions need another member to second them. The motions are debatable (in terms of being in the committee, not the content of the motion in the committee) and are also amendable. The chair should ask if there is any discussion, and a vote should be taken. If the motion to discharge the committee is adopted, then there can be action on the main motion that had been sent to the committee. It can be discussed immediately.

Reconsidering a Motion

Is there a change of mind about a matter that was voted upon? It's possible to reconsider a motion, with some important cautions: If your group's or organization's meeting takes place in one day (or less), the motion to reconsider must be made the same day.

Members who are in a convention or session can reconsider during the next day. Has more time elapsed? Then members should use the motion to rescind or amend something previously adopted. Finally, if the motion has been defeated at a previous meeting, members can always think about renewing a motion by changing it and reintroducing it to the membership as new business.

 ESSENTIAL

> If too much time elapsed and it's too late to reconsider a motion, action on the motion will proceed unless the membership decides to make a motion to rescind or amend something previously adopted.

Which Side Were You On?

Because the motion to reconsider keeps all other business at a standstill until it's taken care of, in order to prevent its being used by a member to cause problems, only a member who voted on the prevailing side will be allowed to introduce it. The chair must ask the member if she was on the prevailing side if the member doesn't state this in her request.

Making the Motion

If a member wants to make a motion to reconsider, he should say, "I move to reconsider the vote on the motion to [do such-and-such]. I voted on the prevailing side." Another member needs to second the motion. Then the chair should ask if there is any discussion on reconsidering the vote. After discussion (if any), a new vote will be taken.

The motion is debatable *if* the type of motion it reconsiders is debatable. It can't be reconsidered (actually, that would be re-reconsidering it, wouldn't it?). (See Appendix B for the list of debatable and nondebatable motions.) If adopted, the original motion is put before the membership as if there had never been a vote upon it previously.

 FACT

> The motion to reconsider cannot be made if the original motion has been carried out (or partially carried out), if something can't be redone, if some other motion can get the same result, or if something like a contract has been made with another party or a notification has been made to a member or someone outside the group or organization.

Reconsider and Enter on the Minutes

What if some members want to reconsider something at a meeting where they find themselves at a temporary advantage? They may know—even if they pretend otherwise!—that their view is contrary to that of the majority of the members, but they want their way. An example of this might happen when there's been an overlong meeting and many members have headed home, not realizing that a quorum still exists—a quorum of members who want the group or organization to do something the majority doesn't support.

Hey, Come Back!

You look around and you don't spot any other members who voted on the prevailing side of the motion. What can one member do? Well, you can make a motion to "reconsider and enter on the minutes the vote on [X topic]."

Here's the sticky part: No matter how you voted on the motion previously, you need to vote *for* the motion the rest of the members are pushing because *only then,* when you are on the prevailing side, can you raise a motion to reconsider. If there's a second, action on what was proposed to be reconsidered is suspended. Then the other members can be notified to be present when the matter is brought up for reconsideration at the next meeting.

Help Is on the Way

What if no one in the temporary minority voted on the prevailing side? And what if it's too late for any member to change her vote? There's a way for this to be fixed. Notice should be sent to members by mail or e-mail or fax that a motion to rescind the vote will be made at the group's or organization's next meeting, and there, a true majority will have the chance to vote on the motion to rescind.

Learning a Lesson

You see why seasoned members of groups have learned to stay until the final minutes of a meeting? They've become wise to the fact that you never know when there will be members who try to get away with something that they are very well aware the majority doesn't support! If members need to leave a meeting before it's adjourned, they should make certain that at least a few members on their side (the majority position) of issues are there to play watchdog.

 ALERT!

> The chair should be alert to a failure to call up a motion to reconsider. If the time for adjournment is at hand and the motion to reconsider addressed something that must be done before the next meeting, then the chair must point out the situation so the membership can act.

Isn't it nice to know that just because your group or organization voted on something, it's not cast in stone, so to speak? With the motions in this chapter, you and others have the power to change what's taken place in previous meetings. You have the information you need whether you want to rescind, amend something that's previously adopted, reconsider, or "head off the bad guys" when they try something sneaky with your motion to reconsider and enter on the minutes. They're great motions to help you and other members vote with confidence, knowing that if information comes to light that merits changing some previous action, it may be possible to do so.

Chapter 11

Renewing and Refusing Motions

As you know, the membership of a group or organization can't be asked to look at a motion twice in the same meeting. If it weren't for this rule, imagine how members could make a meeting seem like a merry-go-round, constantly proposing and reproposing a motion over and over again in the very same meeting. That's why restrictions have been placed on the process of renewing motions, and why safeguards have been built in to prevent members from trying to use dilatory (delaying) tactics and improper motions.

How and When to Renew

When a motion has been made but the membership disposed of it without adopting it and a member brings it up again, the motion is considered to be renewed. In Chapter 10 you learned several ways to reconsider a motion: bringing up a motion to reconsider a vote, a motion to rescind an action, or amending something already adopted may be your Lazarus tools to bring a motion back to life. Changing the wording of the motion can also help breathe life back into a motion and some-times help get it passed. As with many things, timing is everything.

Timing

Did a member make a motion and then withdraw it? Timing is everything. There may be many good rea-sons why the member did this. She may have realized that others just aren't in the mood for what she was proposing at the moment, a quorum isn't present yet, a certain faction seems very much in evidence and poten-tial backers of the motion aren't present yet—any number of factors could exist.

For whatever reason, the member withdrew the motion. Does this mean the motion can't be brought up again? The answer is no. It's as if the motion never happened to begin with. Enter the motion, withdraw the motion, re-enter the motion.

ESSENTIAL

> Some parliamentary experts feel renewing a motion is more efficient than reconsidering a motion that has been voted down. Changing the wording and trying again can be easier than finding support for reconsidering a motion. Sometimes there's a bothersome phrase that has disturbed members; rewording it and renewing it might make it successful.

Okay, Let's Renew It!

Motions that can be renewed at the same meeting or session are those that have been withdrawn before members did anything to them; motions that have substantial wording changes; or motions to commit or to postpone definitely, to limit or extend debate, to order the previous question, to take from the table, to call for the orders of the day, to recess, and to adjourn.

There Are Conditions (Of Course)

Some groups and organizations don't allow the renewing of motions during the meeting at which they were originally proposed. They may have experienced problems with members doing this in the past and have put wording into their bylaws to guard against renewing. Be sure you check your bylaws first. If you've checked and renewing a motion is allowed, then you can proceed.

Main motions without a change, amendments to a motion, or a motion to postpone indefinitely *cannot* be renewed at the same meeting or session.

Renewing a Motion

It's the chair's responsibility to make certain that the motion that a member wants to renew has a difference in the wording or the time or circumstance. Of course, a withdrawn motion can be proposed again. The chair should listen carefully to the motion being made verbally, or should read the motion if it's in writing, to verify that the renewed motion has been changed as the member maintains it has.

Resolutions Can Be Renewed, Too

A member might want to renew a resolution; if so, the resolution should have changes in wording or time or circumstance. If a list of resolutions was proposed and failed to get an affirmative majority vote, it might be that one resolution is what made the whole list fail. The discussion prior to voting may make it clear which resolution was not liked, or a check of other members may reveal this information. Then, a member could present the list again, leaving out that one bothersome resolution. This way, the motion will be changed enough to make it again, and it may have a better chance of being adopted.

Making the Motion

To make a motion to renew, a member should use the same procedure that would be used to propose a new motion ("I move that [we do X]" and so on). The chair should make certain that another member makes a motion to second, and that there is debate, if it's desired. Then a vote should be taken. A majority vote in the affirmative is required for adoption.

 ESSENTIAL

> Be observant. Watch nonverbal messages that people are sending during meetings. Smiles and nodding signal agreement or approval, while frowns and shaking heads show disagreement or disapproval. These cues can help give you information that may make you—and your motions—more successful.

What Are You Trying to Do?

What if a member who isn't well versed in Robert's Rules—or who chooses to bend them to what he wants them to be—tries to ram a motion through by saying that it's been reworded, when, really, it sounds like the same old motion? The chair—or a member, if the chair doesn't notice—needs to call this to the attention of the membership. Someone might also try to renew a motion to reconsider or rescind that has been voted down, and that attempt needs to be rejected as well unless the motion has been substantially changed.

If a member has raised a point of order or a question of privilege and the chair has ruled against it, it can be raised again only if an appeal is successful and the chair's decision is reversed. If the chair's decision is sustained, however, a point of order or a question of privilege can't be made again during the meeting.

 FACT

> No motion can be renewed while the vote on it can be reconsidered. It would be redundant to waste time making another motion while the original one can be reconsidered with a vote.

Progress Changes the Rules

Perhaps your meeting has gone along for some time and there's been a lot of business conducted. Some subsidiary motions such as commit, postpone to a certain time, limit or extend limits of debate for the previous question, and lay on the table can be renewed if a meeting has advanced or debate over a motion has made it to where they are different questions (motions). Something unexpected or urgent could also come up that the membership was not aware of at the beginning of the meeting; if the members had made a motion to lay on the table and it was rejected, it could be renewed.

Renewal of a motion is always allowed at a later meeting unless your group or organization has postponed it to the current meeting and not considered it yet. Obviously, this is because it hasn't come up yet!

You Just Couldn't Budge Them

Members may have wanted to stay with whatever they were discussing and refused to proceed to the orders of the day when a member proposed they should do so. The motion to proceed to the orders of the day can be renewed when the business is concluded (and maybe members won't reject it this time). Likewise, members may not have wanted to adjourn or recess. But after more time (or a long, long speech?), they might be more inclined to want to do this. Then a motion to renew either adjourn or recess can be made.

Did I Hear a Nomination?

If your group or organization is discussing nominations, motions to close or reopen them can be renewed. The renewal can take place after there has been a lot of debate or progress in the nomination process, so they are really new questions (motions). More information on nominations and elections can be found in Chapter 14.

When You Can't Renew

If the motion has been laid on the table, it's still there at the next meeting, so you can't renew it yet. If a committee hasn't been reported yet, there can't be a motion to renew the matter that was sent there until after the meeting at which the committee was supposed to report. And if a motion has been put under some sort of reconsideration that hasn't been taken care of (or it's expired while waiting for reconsideration), it can't be renewed.

 ALERT!

Maybe you've made a motion to adjourn but no one else wants to. So you wait, and more business is transacted. Be sure that it's sufficient business, not something like a motion to recess or lay on the table. That's not considered enough business to renew a motion to adjourn.

If a member has made an objection to consideration of a question and it wasn't sustained, it can't be renewed with that main motion if it goes to another session. This is because an objection to consideration of a question is raised when the main motion is introduced and before any consideration of it. However, if the main motion is voted down or it's postponed indefinitely and then renewed at the next meeting, it's now a new motion—and members are free to object to it again.

Disruptive Tactics

If the purpose of a motion is to hinder or impede the will of the membership, it's considered to be *dilatory*.

Since the purpose of using Robert's Rules is the good of all members, the chair must be vigilant about possible abuse of parliamentary procedure. In particular, the chair should be watchful for members attempting to renew motions just to hinder or impede business and the will of the membership.

Send out the Clowns

Obviously, if a motion is absurd, it doesn't have any place in the running of a serious group or organization. There's nothing funny about members who become so disgruntled with what is happening as business is conducted that they try to disrupt meetings by raising points of order, appealing the decisions of the chair, or making motions that do nothing but delay or deter the addressing of important matters. Imagine the frustration other members would experience, not to mention the waste of time and energy on the part of everyone attending the meeting. Business could come to a complete halt.

 QUESTION?

What if you're not sure if a motion is deliberately obstructive?
Then the chair must assume that the motion has been made in good faith, and behave accordingly. It's better to give the maker of the motion the benefit of the doubt and let the membership help defeat it.

Rain on Their Parade

When we talk about members who are trying to obstruct action, we're not talking about those who simply aren't with the mainstream of most of the membership; most of us have some opinions that run counter to those of others on any given day. We're talking about members who use and abuse parliamentary procedure as a way to be obstructive and feel powerful as a result of their actions. What can a chair do with these deliberately obstructive members?

First, the chair can refuse to recognize these members or he can rule against their motions. It's important that the chair never let personal feelings cloud his judgment in making rulings. Fairness and firmness should be the guiding principles in dealing with obstructive members; if these members become unruly, then that's a different matter.

Improper Motions

Improper motions are those that run counter to something already decided—that is, they disagree with a motion which has been voted upon at the same meeting. For example, a group or organization votes to spend money to improve the clubhouse, then, at the same meeting, someone makes a motion to disallow spending of club money on the clubhouse—this is a motion that runs counter. Making a motion with wording so similar to another motion already voted upon that it's just a waste of time or confusing to members also runs counter. Sometimes they conflict with adopted or rejected motions. *Improper* doesn't necessarily refer to the content of the motion, but rather to the method that the maker is using, which could be an attempt to disrupt the will of the membership.

Motions can also be improper if they deal with a motion that has been referred to a committee that hasn't reported yet. In addition, if a motion has been postponed to a certain time, it's improper to make another motion with the same content. A motion is also improper if it is the same as a motion subject to reconsider.

 FACT

> One of the most frequently used improper "motions" is "table a motion." There is no such motion. Sometimes a member tries to use this phrase to kill a motion. However, a motion can't be disposed of this way. A member could make the motion to postpone indefinitely or, if it's just that the timing is wrong, make a motion to postpone the motion to a specific time.

Any motion that runs counter to the corporate charter, constitution, bylaws, or other rules of a group or organization is improper. It is also improper to make motions that conflict with the U.S. Constitution or state constitutions, or with national, state, or local laws. In short, no one should be making motions in your group or organization that are illegal within it or contrary to the laws of this country.

If a motion is outside the object of your group or organization as it has been defined in the bylaws, it can't be considered unless two-thirds of the membership agrees to consider it. Also, motions can't have language that slanders or libels a member's conduct or character. Likewise, motions that are overly harsh, rude, or not allowed in debate (such as questioning the motives of a member in debate) are improper.

Calling a Member to Task

Is there a member—even worse, several members—who has been disrupting meetings with improper motions? Has this been happening frequently? Do other members seem to be tiring of this but don't know how to proceed?

Sometimes a difference of opinion about the direction a group or organization is heading in will suddenly spring up. A single issue begins to divide the group. Sometimes, it's something that's been simmering for a long time that is just now coming to a head. Other times, there is a faction of discontented members that is unwilling to work in a cooperative, cohesive manner within the group, and unwilling to go off and form its own group.

Why Not Leave?

It's tradition you're trampling on, and we must keep things as they are, this faction seems to be saying.

That's why it is trying to hold off progress by obstructing business with improper motions and disruptive behavior. Or, it claims to have "been here first" and it has no intention of leaving the group. Sometimes a faction can claim to be trying to bring "new blood" or "fresh air" into the organization and doesn't understand why its actions aren't appreciated. Some groups and organizations have even split into two or more individual groups because of these differences.

Steps to Take

Members can convey a sense of support for a chair who is in a difficult position, fending off these improper motions. It needn't be—probably shouldn't be—displayed in an obvious way. But it's always appreciated. The chair should also continue to deflect improper motions; explaining why the motions are improper might go a long way toward preventing future abuses. Finally, staying calm and composed will effectively show offending members that they won't win with intimidation.

Officers and members who know how to renew motions and avoid making improper motions according to Robert's Rules are worth their weight in gold in a group or organization. So much time is saved and so much more business can be conducted when the proper parliamentary procedure is used in meetings. There's nothing worse than having to sit through a meeting where members stumble and fumble over the rules. An added bonus occurs when members use the rules in the spirit that they are intended to be used—for the greater good of those involved. When this happens, you don't just have good groups and organizations, you have great ones.

 ESSENTIAL

It *is* possible that a member who makes a number of improper motions may not be doing so deliberately, but may simply not be up to speed on Robert's Rules. In this case, another member could approach the one who is making the improper motions outside the meeting and quietly talk to her, offering some advice on Robert's Rules and parliamentary procedure.

Chapter 12

Who Has the Floor?

Being heard and being allowed to participate are the principles at the heart of Robert's Rules. Debate is an integral part of parliamentary procedure. A member who wishes to speak must be recognized by the chair, which means that she is given the floor. More importantly, if a member is not given the floor, she has no voice in the democratic process of the group or organization. This chapter covers what you need to know about debating a motion.

Allowing for Debate

Debate is essential for a deliberative assembly, but if you don't follow Robert's Rules, debate can become unproductive or unpleasant—or both. Relying on the rules can help maintain order so that a more democratic exchange of ideas and action can take place.

As you know, once a motion is made, members debate it. The maker of the motion goes first, then others may respond. (Your bylaws should contain a provision as to how long one member may speak, to avoid the problem of one person monopolizing time.)

Debate should center on the motion, not diverge into other areas. Remarks that malign the member speaking or question why he is making the motion should absolutely not be allowed. The chair does not usually enter into debate unless the organization meeting is a small committee or group.

 ALERT!

> Your bylaws should contain a provision as to how long one member may speak, to avoid the problem of one person monopolizing the debate. Ten minutes is the preferred limit, but this may be too much or too little time for your group, depending on its size.

A good chair will not only remain impartial in a debate, but will openly encourage debate on both sides of an issue. The chair can accomplish this by inviting the members to "speak for the motion" or "speak against the motion." When the chair does this, she is modeling democratic behavior, and she's also making certain that debate doesn't become one-sided.

It's a good rule to follow to have the chair explain exactly what will happen with a vote for or against a motion. This helps clarify the consequences of a motion for everyone up front. The vote is then taken and announced. (More about the mechanics of voting in Chapter 13.)

Determining Who Speaks

A member who wishes to speak in debate must obtain the floor. This means that the chair must "recognize" the member, that is, give him the exclusive right to be heard at the time of the request. It can't be stressed enough that the chair must remember to always recognize a member entitled to the floor; maintaining a reputation of fairness is essential not only to the office of chair, but also to the atmosphere of idealism a good group or organization should strive to cultivate.

A member should rise and, if no other member has the floor, address the chair. If the meeting is being held in a large room and there is a microphone, she should go to it to speak. Otherwise, the member can stand next to the chair she was occupying and speak. (In some small groups, members stay seated.)

The first member to rise should be the one recognized by the chair. If it's a small group where everyone knows everyone else, the chair can simply nod and the member is given the floor and may speak. If the group is larger, the chair and/or others may not know the member's name. If so, the member should state it, the chair repeats it, and then the member may speak.

There Are Two of Us Standing

What if two members attempt to obtain the floor at the same time? The member who rose and addressed the chair first after the floor was yielded (given up) is the one who should be recognized.

 ALERT!

> A member can't gain an advantage by beginning to rise or by rising before the floor has been yielded by the current speaker. You must wait until the current speaker is finished. Courtesy and fairness should prevail at all times.

There are times when another member may stand and, in effect, interrupt by rising before the floor is yielded. While the list is not short, remember that these accepted interruptions are not to be taken lightly—they are fairly serious or urgent reasons to interrupt a speaker. Accepted interruptions include calling a member to order, or calling for the orders of the day, the division of the assembly, a parliamentary inquiry, a point of information, or a point of order.

It's also permissible to raise a question of privilege, an appeal, or an objection to the consideration of a question. If a member has been assigned the floor but hasn't started to speak, there are a few reasons she may be interrupted, including giving notice of intent to introduce a motion requiring notice or making a motion to reconsider or to reconsider and enter on the minutes.

As you can see, most of these matters, while important, could probably wait until the speaker is finished speaking—unless there is a sudden emergency and the meeting room needs to be vacated!

Who's on First?

When the membership has a motion open to debate, there are three times when the floor should be given to a member who was not the first to rise but who actually rose before another member was recognized. Perhaps the member who made the motion chose not to speak right away but has decided she wants to do so now. That member must be recognized first.

No member may speak twice in debate if there are any members who have not had the opportunity to speak, so the member(s) who has not done so would have priority over any other speakers. After all, democracy must prevail. No member should be allowed to monopolize a meeting, or individual rights have not been maintained.

And finally, if the chair knows that there are members who have opinions at the opposite ends of the spectrum, he can choose to alternate speakers between those in favor of and those opposed to a matter.

 ALERT!

The chair recognized the wrong person. Maybe the room is large and the chair doesn't realize he or she has called on the person who stood second, not the first. The chair has made an error. The wronged member can call the chair's attention to the mistake by raising a point of order. The chair should then correct the mistake.

Giving Preference

While in general one member shouldn't be given preferential treatment over another, there are times when doing this is in the interest of the membership. If several members rise at once (which is certain to happen sometimes in a large group, or one that tends to move at a fast pace), the chair could start to feel like she has several jack-in-the-box toys. It's important for the chair to take the members and their requests for the floor in the order of importance. The situations described here are discussed in order from highest priority to lowest.

When debate is pending, it's acceptable for a member to rise and give previous notice of another motion. Is there is a motion to put into effect a recommendation made by a committee? Then the committee member who presented the report should be given preference to speak.

If a member made a motion to take a question from the table, that member may also be given preference to speak. Also, a member who made a motion to reconsider (not always the one who called it up) should be given preference, as should a member who moves to reconsider a vote on a motion to amend a motion.

When Debate Is Not Allowed

If the question pending isn't debatable, a member can be given the floor only if he wants to give previous notice of a motion or make a motion or raise a question that takes precedence over the question that's pending at the moment. If members want to amend the undebatable motion, the person who made the motion to reconsider gets preference to the floor.

For a list of debatable and nondebatable motions, see Appendix B.

When No Question Is Pending

Perhaps there is a time when there is no pending question during the meeting. The group or organization has moved on a motion that needs other motions to accomplish its purpose. At this time, a member may have preference to the floor to continue the series of motions. The chair should let this member proceed, even if another member rose and addressed the chair first.

For example, if something urgent came up, a member might ask to lay the current motion on the table. After the urgent matter was handled, it's back to the motion on the table. The member who asked to put it on the table should be given preference to resurrect it and see it through.

 QUESTION?

What if you've just discovered a committee has been appointed, but some important details have been left out of the motion that they have been appointed to study?
Relax! It's not too late to fix the situation. The member who proposed the motion doesn't get preference, but *nothing new is introduced* until the membership takes care of the committee problem by amending the original motion.

Another time that a member gets preference to recognition is when rules have been suspended in order to bring up and take action on a motion. Once those rules are suspended, of course, this member should be allowed to make the motion itself.

A member might urge others to vote down a motion because she felt a better motion could be offered. After the original motion has been defeated, this member gets preference to propose what she feels is a better motion. (Be sure that the motion is different enough from the first, because two motions that are alike can't be voted on in one meeting.)

There might be a situation when there is no question pending, and a member might rise to make a main motion. Another member will get preference to the floor if he or she rises to say he or she wants to make a motion to reconsider and enter on the minutes, moves to reconsider a vote, calls up a motion to reconsider, or moves to take a question from the table when it's correct to do this.

Confused? Let the Members Decide!

If you're the chair and you're ready to tear your hair out trying to get it all straight about who gets preference to the floor, relax! You can delegate this responsibility if you wish. Simply allow the membership to make a decision with a vote. The member with the most votes gets to go first with his or her motion. Plain and simple.

 ESSENTIAL

It's possible to raise a point of order if there's been a mistake in assigning the floor to the wrong member in a regular meeting. However, during mass meetings or conventions, whether one person gets precedence over another really has to take second place to important business. No appeal should be made to the chair.

Length of Debates

When the membership of a group or organization discusses a pending question, it's said to debate it. The principle of debate is essential to Robert's Rules and the democratic process. Every member has the right to debate any motion that is debatable. This right is so important that to take it away at any time, the membership must vote and have a two-thirds majority in favor to make the change.

Timing Debate

There are rules for debate, including how often a member can speak and for how long. The first and most basic rule is that there cannot be debate on a motion until it has been made. This will save time for the membership because a motion may not be popular and may die without a second; if there had been discussion first, it would have been wasted in this situation.

Debate must wait, too, for the maker of the motion to speak. After this has been done, it's time for members to speak for or against the motion. Some groups and organizations, particularly if they are large, have restrictions on debate written into their bylaws. Members have learned that if everyone speaks, it would take far too long to conduct business. Those who wish to speak twice may do so, but not until all have had a chance to speak first.

Hey, I'm Not Finished!

It's not only rude, but incorrect in parliamentary procedure for the chair to become impatient and try to get a vote going before all members have been given their opportunity to speak in debate. Are there many members who wish to speak and it's running late? Perhaps if you're short on time it would be better to have the membership continue at the next meeting rather than try to rush a motion through.

Two things—maybe more—could happen if you rush a vote. Members could feel slighted, and if enough members feel that their opinions don't matter, that a vote was taken too quickly, there might be a movement to reconsider.

How Much Time Are You in For?

If your group or organization has no rule in its bylaws to limit debate, then members should not be allowed to speak for more than ten minutes *unless* they have the consent of the membership. Is your group small or is this an issue you want to thoroughly explore before voting? Then members can give unanimous consent or members can make a motion to extend the limits of debate, which needs a two-thirds majority vote to pass.

Time's Up!

The chair has a delicate job during debate. She must make certain to be fair and not let a member overrun the time limit. There are also those members who might talk for less than ten minutes and then ask to give their unused time to others, or "bank" the time and use it later. The chair must tactfully but firmly turn down these requests, unless the group or organization allows them in their bylaws (most don't!).

 ESSENTIAL

> Trying to be Mr. or Ms. Nice Member? If you yield to another member for a question, the time that other person uses is *your* time. It's up to you whether you want to give up your time!

Whose Turn to Debate?

Do you like to participate in meetings . . . a lot? Are you the chair of a group or organization full of members who really get involved in debate? Then information on how often members can speak will be very important to you. No member wants to be stopped and told, "You can't speak on the question again today." And the chair certainly doesn't want to be misinformed about the rules and either offend members by stopping them when they deserve another opportunity to speak, or be called to task because he let a member speak too many times.

Unless your bylaws say otherwise, members may speak twice and twice only to the *same* question on the same day, but that second time must not occur until *after* all members have spoken. This ensures that every member has a chance to speak. The rule about speaking twice applies to the same question, not to the entire meeting. Members have the right to speak twice about any amount of questions a day, just never more than twice about the same question. There may be a number of different motions related to the main motion. Each of these can be addressed a total of two times (once, then another time after all members have spoken). So, if, for example, there was a main motion, the member can speak twice, then again twice on a motion to amend the motion, and twice on postponing the motion and . . . well, you get the point!

 FACT

> The exception to the rule about members' not being allowed to speak more than twice to the *same* question on the same day is that of appeal. Members always have the right to appeal without sacrificing their time to speak to a question.

Has a member asked a question? Made a suggestion? Timewise, these are not counted as the member speaking to the question.

If your group or organization decides to continue debate to another meeting and it's on the same day, members who spoke twice at the earlier meeting have effectively finished for the day. A meeting continued to another day gives members a renewed opportunity to speak more because it's a different day.

Modifying Debate Rules

While Robert wrote his rules to help groups and organizations have a uniform method of using parliamentary procedure in their meetings, he was not rigid. He did not urge conformity at the expense of the group's particular need to conduct business with some exceptions to the rules. A group may modify the rules of debate—as it may modify other areas of the rules—to suit its needs.

Does your group want to allow members more time to speak on a debatable question? Or less time? These rules can be modified to suit the group with the adoption of a special rule of order. A two-thirds majority in favor of the change is required for it to be made.

Temporary Change

Perhaps your group doesn't want to change the rules about debate permanently. It's possible to change those rules just for a meeting or session with a main motion (which does not require previous notice). Then there should be a second by another member and a vote; a two-thirds vote in favor will make the change. Conventions usually lend themselves to having stricter limits on debate because they have so much business to conduct in a limited period. If a change in debate rules is desired, modifying is done with a "standing rule of the convention," which requires a two-thirds vote.

Bring It On!

What if your group or organization is really getting into the debate and members seem to want to discard all rules? You don't want a free-for-all, but there is a great technique that can be used so that the members become a community of debaters without the restrictions of how many times a member can speak or for how long, and without waiting until everyone has a chance to speak before a member can speak twice. Your group might want to try resolving itself into a committee of the whole—which means turning the entire membership into a committee, which then can consider the question without restriction. (Remember that when a committee makes a motion, a second is not required before a vote is taken.)

 ALERT!

> No matter how long or short the debate, no matter how many times a member speaks, one thing must always be remembered: Debate must be germane, that is, it must be relevant to the motion.

Stopping or Preventing Debate

When is it time to end the debate? There are a few ways to know. One of these is when members have spoken twice. Another is when debate has gone over the previously agreed-upon time limit. Finally, when the same points keep being repeated and the membership is clearly getting bored and restless, it's time for debate to be over.

Who Stops the Merry-Go-Round?

No one wants to lose members (and thus a quorum) if the debate exceeds the patience limit of most people at the meeting. The chair can't just decide that enough's enough—that could be interpreted as dictatorship. The usual procedure the chair takes is to ask if there are any more members who wish to speak. If it appears that there aren't any, the chair can suggest that the membership entertain a motion to end debate and proceed with a vote.

A member can make a motion to close debate and assist both chair and membership by doing so. To do so, the member should make the previous question or close debate motion. This motion must be seconded by another member, it can't be debated, and it must have a two-thirds vote to adopt. A vote can now proceed.

Preventing Debate Before It Starts

Perhaps while a member is speaking, she decides to conclude with a higher-ranking motion than the one pending. When the chair allows a member to speak, that member may use the floor to make a higher-ranking motion.

What if a member wants to bring up a motion that others just don't want to even think about? They don't want to debate it—they don't want it brought up, period! Don't let her say another word about it, you can almost hear members thinking. What can be done?

Objection to consideration of the question to the rescue! All a member has to do is raise this objection before debate starts or before anyone makes a subsidiary motion. If there's a two-thirds vote, that question is out. It can't be considered in the meeting.

 ESSENTIAL

> Some chairs have members who are on opposing sides of an issue take turns speaking during debate. This makes for a more balanced consideration of an issue and prevents one group from dominating a debate. The chair should ask those who wish to speak which side they will represent. "For" then speaks, followed by "against."

Keeping Debate Peaceful

Once again, courtesy and democratic ideals can't be stressed enough. Members must stay on topic, be polite to each other, and not attack each other verbally or physically. Those who are not speaking should stay quiet and not interrupt. Members are not to address each other in debate; they address the chair. Officers should always be addressed by their title, and members address each other formally, such as by saying, "the member who spoke last" instead of "Mrs. Jones," or, heaven forbid, "that woman who just said the most ridiculous thing."

The chair must stay impartial throughout a debate. She should not speak for or against any motion. To be able to debate, the chair must turn the duty of presiding the meeting over to the vice president of the group or organization, if that individual hasn't spoken on the question. If she has spoken, or if she declines the duty, then the chair may appoint another or nominate a member, which will require a vote.

The chair returns to presiding only when a vote on the pending question has been taken. As you can see, this process should be used sparingly because it can become complicated and can also make the membership begin to doubt the chair's impartiality if she wants to participate in the debate process too often.

 QUESTION?

Can all motions be debated?
No. A list of debatable motions and nondebatable motions is featured in Appendix B of this book.

Handling Transgressions

Sometimes things can get out of hand. A member might make a slanderous remark about, or question the motives of, another. If this happens, the member who is offended should ask the chair to address the matter, or another member may ask the chair to do so. Of course, if there is inappropriate behavior or threats, more serious measures need to be taken.

ESSENTIAL

> In any democratic process, the majority rules. However, it's important to hear the voice of the minority in order to learn, grow, and have the input of all concerned. If the minority is not being heard in your organization, it should be cultivated for the good of all concerned.

Sometimes Bad Behavior Happens

People have strong opinions, especially about matters that are important to them. So it shouldn't come as a surprise that when debate gets heated, tempers may flare and one or more members may speak or act inappropriately. Name-calling, rudeness, disruption of a meeting—any of these and all of these can happen. What should the chair do?

Start with an Easy Step

If the transgression is mild, keep the consequences at a minimum. Robert's Rules are clear that the chair can and must address behaviors in stages. The chair can stand, bang a gavel, or call attention vocally and ask the offending member to be quiet and be seated. If the member continues, the chair should repeat the request for the member to be quiet and be seated.

At this point, it's appropriate for *any* member to make a point of order and ask that the member's behavior be addressed by the chair. Then, the chair can turn to the members and ask what they want done. Notice that the chair does not have the right to levy punishment, but the assembly does. Any member may make a motion to ask the offending member to stop speaking and be seated. If the offending member won't do as requested, a motion may be made to direct that the member be asked to leave the meeting. By a majority vote, the membership can effectively order the member out.

Further Recourse

With luck, none of the above will ever be necessary in a meeting you preside over or attend. However, all of the above behaviors—and worse—have occurred at meetings through the years. If the member's behavior escalates, the chair can ask the secretary to record what the misbehaving member is saying so that the exact words may be read back to the member in later proceedings, as necessary. If this fails to quiet the member or induce her to exit early from the meeting, more serious steps could be taken by the membership.

Many groups that consider controversial issues have resorted to having some form of security in place, whether it's the group's sergeant at arms, a police officer for a city council meeting, or uniformed security at a private meeting. A parent who attends a local school board meeting might see the secretary taking pictures of the assembled audience and speakers, and wonder why. The member who is making a problem of him- or herself is often the one who will create a legal issue, and in a society where litigation is becoming more and more prevalent, making written and photographic records of a problem-making member's behavior is a protection many groups are taking.

 QUESTION?

What if a member's misbehavior happens outside an official meeting?
Depending on the nature of the offense, the membership can prefer (press) charges and hold a trial *in executive session*—nothing must be made public of this trial. If the member is found guilty, the group may expel her but may not make publicly known the charge.

As you can see, the member who is recognized has a lot of power to make things happen. She can speak for or against a motion and influence other members and, thus, their vote. Having limits on how often a member may speak, and for how long, protects that invaluable right to debate so that all may participate in an orderly and democratic way. Know your rights to be recognized and speak and you have become an invaluable member or officer of your group or organization.

Chapter 13
Let's Vote!

What's more democratic than voting? It's the cornerstone of American democracy. Robert's Rules set out specific recommendations for protecting the individual member's right to vote in groups and organizations. Whether your group is large or small, civic or social, voting is integral to conducting business and furthering the goals of the group. No business can be conducted without voting. No officers can be elected without voting. And there is no integrity in a group or organization that does not vigorously guard the fairness and impartiality of the voting process.

Why Vote?

We've all heard the question: Why vote? We've all probably asked ourselves that question at some point in our lives. Sometimes it just doesn't seem like it matters. Maybe we're feeling a bit cynical about the outcome, that our one vote doesn't matter. It's been a long day, a long week of long days, actually, and who wants to sit in that meeting and cast that vote when you know everyone's going to vote the opposite way you are. What's the point? you find yourself asking.

Or you're at that meeting and you have enthusiasm for what's happening. But the time for the vote arrives and you're not sure you know which way to vote. Persuasive arguments have been made on both sides. What if you vote the wrong way? You decide not to vote.

 FACT

> No one *has* to vote. Just as you have a right to vote in your group or organization, so, too, you have the right not to vote. When the vote is counted, it's the number of votes cast, not how many members are present that are counted, unless your group's bylaws say otherwise.

Before you skip out on the meeting, remember why you joined that group or organization. And remember that one vote *does* matter. It might be the one that breaks a tie that night. A majority vote is more than half of the votes cast, and yours might be the deciding factor. That motion, that election, might be a very important one for the group you care about.

Not voting might look like a solution. But it can be the same as voting against something. That majority or two-thirds vote in favor might not pass with your blank vote or your abstention. It's a good idea to vote.

Who Can Vote

Each member is entitled to one vote. This vote can't be taken away until the member has voluntarily left the group, has been dropped from it, or is under a disciplinary suspension. While Robert's Rules maintain that members who are in arrears with their dues still have voting rights, some groups have found it necessary to prohibit such members from voting. As always, check your group's bylaws for more information.

Group officers have the same voting rights as members do. Since the chair should always maintain an impartial presence, he or she might choose to vote only in certain circumstances. These would include when there is a secret ballot or when it will affect the outcome of an election, such as by breaking a tie so that a motion can pass, creating a tie that will defeat a motion, or being the deciding ballot in a two-thirds vote.

Voting Procedures

There is no one procedure that is right for all types of groups or organizations. If your group is small, a voice vote or a show of hands might be appropriate. However, these procedures can be problematic for larger groups, which may use a rising vote. If there may be closeness on a vote that might lead to a question of its accuracy, then additional safeguards like a rising vote or roll call need to be implemented.

How It Works

The chair chooses the way that the group will vote, whether by voice, hand, or rising vote, but any member may make a motion regarding how a vote will be taken. The member should say, "I move that the vote on this motion be taken by a show of hands" or "I move that the vote on this motion be taken by members rising and being counted" or "I move that the vote on this motion be taken by roll call." This motion needs to have a second, it can't be debated, and it requires a majority vote.

 ESSENTIAL

> A member should not vote on any motion in which she has a personal or financial interest and there is no such benefit to other members. A member *can* vote on a motion if it contains her name as well as the names of other members.

If the vote is to be taken by voice vote or a show of hands, the chair should first explain to the members what the effects of an "aye" and a "no" vote are. The chair must stand so that he can fully see the membership and make certain that a quorum exists: Otherwise, taking a vote is unnecessary (because it would be invalid). Next, the chair should call for the affirmative vote, then the negative vote. Then the chair should announce the result of the vote and tell the membership whether the motion has passed or been defeated.

Remember General Consent

Don't forget that general consent (also sometimes called universal consent) is a great shortcut that can save a lot of time and effort in voting. There must be general agreement among group members. General consent can be used for every aspect of voting during your meetings, from approving minutes to approving payment of bills to elections of officers and committee members.

Just because members go along with general consent doesn't mean that they are in complete agreement, just that they choose not to object—they may have decided to choose their battles and save objections for the issues that matter more to them. If there are members who don't want to go along with general consent, all they have to do is object and then the item in question will be put to a vote.

Voting by Ballot

When it's important that a member's vote be private, a written ballot is the proper choice. Is a motion controversial? Do some members fear some sort of unpleasantness, even a backlash or retaliation if their vote is known? Members *do* have the right to make a motion to conduct the vote by written ballot.

How It's Done

A ballot is simply a small piece of paper that may or may not be prepared ahead of time. Perhaps a matter comes up that the membership decides should be voted on in secrecy. If a ballot hasn't been prepared before the meeting, a member would simply write "yes" or "no" on the paper.

 ALERT!

> Some parliamentarians caution that members should not get to cut a piece of paper for their own ballot because it has led to voting irregularities in the past (that's a euphemism for cheating!). To be on the safe side, it's best for the secretary or chair to distribute a ballot (even if it is blank) for members to write their vote on.

Is there time to prepare a ballot before the meeting? An example of a question on a ballot prepared ahead of time might be, "Shall the club pay for three members to attend the annual conference in Memphis? Circle Yes or No." (Alternately, members could place an *X* in a blank marked "Yes" or "No".)

It Goes in This Box

Ballots can be gathered in several ways. The members who pass out, collect, and tabulate the ballots are called tellers. In large groups or organizations, they may be part of a tellers' committee.

Members can place their ballots in a ballot box that sits near two tellers in the front of the meeting room. The ballots can also be handed to a teller, who then has the opportunity to feel the ballots to make certain that members have not tried to put two or more ballots in the box. Or one teller may pass a ballot box for members to put their ballots inside and have another teller follow behind to make certain no one casts more than one ballot.

The tellers give the results of the vote to the chair, who then announces it. These tellers should be members who can be trusted to be fair and accurate. In a controversial situation, especially a hotly contested election, tellers representing both sides of the debate should be appointed.

Neither Rain Nor Snow Nor Computer Glitches . . .

Do the bylaws state that ballots for elections and amendments to the bylaws can be sent and received by mail? Then there should be language inserted in the bylaws to detail how this is to be handled.

Some groups have also found that voting that has been done by mail in the past can be done by e-mail. This should be done only if the sender uses an e-mail program that will request a return receipt by the ballot recipient. No one wants a glitch to prevent some members from getting their ballot—or at least saying they didn't when they did!—and challenging the election. Instructions on how to respond should be included.

 ALERT!

Convenience can spell problems when using e-mail for votes. E-mail will take away the ability of members to have a secret vote, because as the votes come into the teller's e-mail inbox, they have the senders' name/e-mail name on them.

Majority Vote

The majority rules in any democratic group or organization. So it follows that a majority vote is required to approve actions or choices by the membership of a group or organization. A majority is more than half, so a majority vote is more than half of the members present who are legally entitled to vote. As stated previously, a quorum is the number of members who must be in attendance to conduct business. This number is usually dictated by the bylaws of your group or organization.

Computing the Majority Vote

It's simple to compute a majority vote. A majority is one more than half of the quorum needed to conduct business. For example, if the quorum needed is fifty members, a majority vote must be twenty-six. Abstentions (a member feels there is a reason to refrain from voting) and blank ballots don't count. The members who vote (which doesn't always mean the number of members present) determine the majority.

Tie Votes

Whoops! It's a tie! The membership is evenly divided and there has not been a majority vote. If the chair hasn't voted, now's the time to break the tie—remembering that he can't vote once as a member and again as a presiding officer. He gets only one vote, just like any other member. If the vote was taken by ballot, however, the chair has already voted and can't vote again to break the tie. A tie vote fails. Another vote should be taken.

Majority Modifications

A group or organization may decide that it wants to modify its requirement for a majority vote to say "a majority of those present" or "a majority of the entire membership." The latter term may mean more than half of those present are required to vote. Here is an example using the formula of a group that has a quorum requirement of fifty. If the group's membership consists of seventy-five individuals and you specified a requirement of "a majority of the entire membership," the number of votes required to pass would be thirty-eight, not twenty-six, which constitutes a simple majority. It might be harder to achieve thirty-eight votes for approval than twenty-six votes.

 ALERT!

> Make certain that anytime a "majority vote" is mentioned it's clear whether *majority* means a majority of those present or a majority of the entire membership. The two terms are very different things.

Your group can make modifications in the voting requirements in its bylaws. Its members can also use a motion to change the voting requirements on a onetime basis at a meeting. Since this action takes away the rights of members, it's necessary to have given previous notice. There must have been an announcement made that there would be a change in the voting procedure at the next meeting.

It's also possible for your group to write the bylaws to require a three-fourths vote if it wishes. Sometimes members prefer that certain types of business or elections be subject to a three-fourths vote. However, most groups and organizations find the simple majority vote to be the best option for them.

The Two-Thirds Vote

A two-thirds vote is required to pass motions that could take away the rights of members. For instance, a two-thirds vote is required to limit or close debate because it prevents members from continuing to speak or it limits how long they can speak. This can seriously affect a vote if more information or opinions are needed for members to make up their minds.

Likewise, any motion that prevents introduction of a motion should require a two-thirds vote. This is because it is an attempt to stop a member (and the membership) from consideration of something that could be very important.

It's important to have a two-thirds vote to suspend or modify a rule or order that the members have previously adopted. That first action was probably given a lot of consideration. In light of that, most people would probably agree that it should take some doing to undo something that has already been passed under careful consideration.

 ESSENTIAL

> The chair does not have to vote. But if he decides to, it's not a good idea to have members know his vote, since the chair is supposed to be impartial. If the chair does vote, it's best to do it by secret ballot.

A two-thirds vote is also required for the weighty task of taking away membership or an office. Membership has obviously been important to a person or he wouldn't have joined. For whatever reason a group or organization decides to take away membership, it should be something that is supported by more than just a few members who might have a grudge.

Taking away an office is a very serious step, one that might change a person's standing in her personal life, her work, and her community. The decision to do this should come from as many members as possible.

When Two-Thirds Is Necessary

Matters that require a two-thirds vote are very important. As you can see from the following list, there are many cases in which a two-thirds vote is necessary to pass a motion. A two-thirds vote is required to:

Limit or close debate.
Suspend or modify a rule or order previously adopted.
Prevent the introduction of a motion.
Take away membership or office.
Amend or rescind something previously adopted,
    if notice hasn't been sent.
Close nominations; close the polls.
Discharge a committee (if notice has not been given).
Extend time for consideration of pending question
    or time until scheduled adjournment or recess.
Make a special order.
Call to vote on the motion pending (previous question).
Refuse to proceed to the orders of the day.
Suspend the rules.
Take up a question out of its proper order.
Take up an order of the day before the time for
    which it has been set.

Calculating the Vote

If sixty members vote, a two-thirds vote is forty. If there are twice as many votes for as against, that's a two-thirds vote. If you're in charge of certifying a vote and you're concerned about making a mistake in math, carry along a calculator. Using it will only take a moment. Don't worry that doing so will make you look stupid. Instead, you'll be demonstrating how important an accurate vote count is, something that is vital to your group's integrity.

 QUESTION?

Are you unsure of the count?
If the chair doubts the accuracy of the vote he has just taken, especially if it was a voice vote in a large group, the chair should take a rising vote. This will demonstrate very clearly what the correct vote is for all concerned.

The Plurality Vote

A candidate or proposition that wins the largest number of votes when three (or more) choices are available is said to have the plurality. Notice how this is different from a majority, where more than half the votes is the deciding factor. Some groups and organizations allow plurality votes in their elections because they have found that it's not possible to elect officers by majority vote. Perhaps no candidate strikes the members in such a way that he is the overwhelming favorite.

Look at Those Bylaws

If there has been a problem getting a majority vote in the past for one candidate, having provisions in the bylaws for a plurality vote might be a good idea. If your group doesn't have such provisions and you've had a problem achieving majority votes in an election, consider a change in the bylaws. Some groups, particularly large ones that use a mail vote, have found plurality votes save time and money when majority votes failed and elections had to be conducted again—at great expense if mail ballots were to be used.

Doubting or Disputing the Vote

The chair announces the vote, and if no one doubts or disputes the result, then the vote stands, and it is recorded in the minutes. If, however, a member has a doubt about the accuracy of the results, that's a different matter. In this case, the member should say, "Division" or "I doubt the result of the vote." Division, an incidental motion, is a procedural question that relates to a pending motion or business, in this case, the vote. It doesn't need a second and it can't be debated.

You've Got the Power

Any member can request that the vote be retaken, and it must be done in a different way. For example, if the vote was taken by voice, it should now be taken by members rising or by a raising of hands or a roll call vote. The chair then announces the vote.

ESSENTIAL

> Requesting a recount is a serious matter. The request should never be made as a spoilsport tactic or to delay proceedings. Unless something really looks wrong, accept the outcome of the vote and move on.

Hopefully this ends it, but if there is continued doubt, a member should ask for a counted vote. This requires a second, is not debatable, and must have a majority vote. To take a counting vote, each member in favor stands and counts off; then each member opposed stands and counts off. Each sits down after he or she counts off. The final vote is then recorded in the minutes.

Doubting the Ballots or Roll Calls

The 2000 presidential election was controversial because of a problem in reading ballots in Florida. In your group or organization, a similar problem could occur with elections for the following reasons: the ballots are unreadable, a candidate didn't meet eligibility requirements, two written ballots were found folded together, or a member voted for two candidates for the same office.

An illegal vote might also have been cast by a noneligible member. And in every group or organization, there always seems to be some jokester who votes for a nonmember. If a member doubts votes by ballot or roll call, he must make a motion to have the tellers' committee recount the vote. The motion must have a majority vote for a recount. The recount stands and the result is recorded in the minutes.

 FACT

An illegal ballot vote doesn't get counted as for or against a candidate. Instead, it's factored into the number that makes up the majority and listed on the teller's report as an illegal ballot. So it's possible that, given unreadable votes and votes for a nonmember, there might not be a candidate who receives a majority vote.

Nothing is more important than voting in furthering the goals of your group or organization. Knowing the rules for voting and keeping elections fair and impartial will help protect the rights of your members. Integrity in all voting matters helps your group maintain its standing and makes you proud to be a member. Under the leadership of Robert's Rules, groups can be minimodels of American democracy.

Chapter 14
I Nominate You

A humor writer once warned her readers not to leave the room while nominations were going on. She said on one occasion she'd left a meeting briefly and returned to find herself in charge of a Girl Scout cookie committee. While it's best not to spring this type of duty on an absent member, there are important rules regarding nominations that you should know about. The process of nominating and electing someone to a position of leadership in your organization should not be conducted carelessly.

Proposing Someone for Office

Election time is nearing. It's time to nominate officers. Some of the current officers may want to continue in their positions. How do you feel about this? What kind of feeling are you getting from other members? Does the membership want to continue with the current leaders? With all of them? Some of them? None of them? Perhaps it's time for a change. And you . . . will you be part of it? Are you the presiding officer? An officer of any sort? Do you want to be?

The Process

How does your group or organization accept nominations? Conduct elections? Do you know? If you've been in your group for a long time, you might be familiar with the process—but not necessarily. It's always best to take a look at your bylaws before the nomination process begins.

Robert's Rules recognize that nominations propose that a person be elected to a particular office. Although many people think of the election itself as the venue of choice, the fact is that the nominating process is where the real choice is made for an office. Think about it: Once you're at the election step, you have a limited number of members from which to choose. In the nominating process, the field is wide open.

ESSENTIAL

> A nominating committee shouldn't be composed of yes-men, members who do anything the current presiding officer wants them to do. Otherwise, the membership will feel betrayed that nominations are being manipulated to suit the current presiding officer.

Do We Need Nominations?

There's no reason for nominations if the same officers who currently serve want to continue and the members want that, too. There's no reason for change if the membership feels that things are running well. Nominations also aren't needed if your group's elections are by ballot or roll call, since members can vote for any member in these processes.

Nomination by Committee

Committees are appointed for the purpose of studying a motion or a matter. They discuss a motion or a matter and save the membership a lot of time and effort within this small group within a group. Nominating committee members can explore the possibilities of candidate choices and their qualifications without the eyes of the entire meeting looking on. They can make recommendations for the best candidate. It's not necessary for them to come up with multiple candidates for each office; they may recommend just one name for each position.

The nominating committee also doesn't have to recommend a name for every officer position. It can leave a position open for nominations from the floor at the regular meeting. Who knows, maybe a member will even volunteer for the position.

Help for the Committee

The nominating committee needs a number of things in order to do its job. It should be given a membership list, the bylaws, eligibility requirements, and a job description for each office. It's very important that the committee members thoroughly discuss whether members they might want to nominate are truly qualified for the positions. Imagine how embarrassing it would be to nominate, and even elect, a member, only to find out that he is not qualified for the position.

The Committee Wants to Talk to You

After the committee has come up with a list of nominations, it's the job of one or more committee members to approach the potential nominees to ask if they're willing to serve. This is an important step that can't be taken lightly. A humor writer can joke about surprise nominations, but members shouldn't be surprised by a nominating committee at a meeting.

Prior notice should always be given. The member has the right to accept or decline being nominated, to not feel pressured and put on the spot in front of her fellow members in a regular meeting. And by the way, it is perfectly acceptable for someone on the nominating committee to be one of those nominated for office.

The Committee Reports

Once the committee has prepared its report, it should be listed on the agenda under "Special Orders." The report is given orally. A list of the nominations can be given to the secretary to record in the minutes.

 ALERT!

> The nominating committee should operate in strict confidence. There should be no leaks of what they've discussed or what nominations will come out of the committee. It should also treat information on membership lists, such as personal information, phone numbers, and addresses, as confidential.

The chair of the nominating committee presents the report by saying, "The nominating committee submits the following nominations: for president, [John Smith]; for vice president, [Jane Doe]; for secretary, [Dan Johnson]; for treasurer [Donna Smith]." Once the report has been given, the committee's job is finished. The committee chair should be seated.

If there has been dissension in the nominating committee, there should be no mention of this at the time of the report at the meeting. If a committee member (or members) didn't get a candidate he wanted on the list of nominations, then he can make a nomination from the floor. Just because a member was on the nominating committee doesn't mean he gives up the right to make a nomination at that time just like any other member.

The Chair Speaks

The chair now accepts the report by restating the list of nominations. Then she should state that nominations are now open from the floor—from the membership. The chair must go through the list from president on down through treasurer, waiting for nominations at each step before proceeding to the next.

Nominations from the Floor

The time has come for members to get in on the process of nominating others for office. As with nominating committees, if you want to nominate someone, ask her in advance if she wants to serve. Some people just hate to be put on the spot!

Speak Up!

Ready to make a nomination from the floor? Members don't have to wait for recognition from the chair to make one. If the group or organization is small, the member doesn't even have to rise to make the nomination. Nominations do not need a second.

There is no reason for nominees to leave the room during the nomination process. It's also unnecessary for them to do so when a vote is taken and then counted. Likewise, the chair doesn't need to step down from presiding over the meeting if she is nominated and the vote is taken and counted.

No, Really, Thank You, But No, Really!

After each nomination, the chair should repeat the name of the person nominated and then ask if there are additional nominations for that office. Has a member been nominated and does not wish to be? She should rise and politely decline while the nominations are still in progress.

 FACT

> Many people don't know that they can nominate themselves for an office. Unfortunately, many people don't have the courage to do this! Think of it as volunteering, and go for it if you feel that you can do a good job. Try to come across as being humble and eager to serve.

Taking Turns

A member can't nominate more than one member for an office until others have had the chance to nominate. This prevents one member from monopolizing the nominations from the floor or from imposing undue influence over other members (who might be intimidated into voting a slate of candidates that she favors).

Nominations can be closed with general consent.

Or, a member can make a motion to close nominations as long as there are no members still trying to make nominations. This motion needs a second, is amendable but not debatable, and requires a two-thirds vote (because it's taking rights from members).

If members decide they want to reopen the nominations, it takes only a majority vote to do this (but still requires a second, and is still amendable but not debatable). Reconsider is still an option with reopening the nominations, but only if there was a negative vote.

Ballot and Mail Nominations

Sometimes a group or organization takes nominations by ballot and by mail instead of by nominating committee or from the floor. Both methods offer members a lot of candor about their choices. By writing it down, members don't have to express their views verbally in a committee or at a meeting. If a ballot is the method for nominations, members will write their nominations on paper, and then a ballot will be drawn up for the members to use in the election.

A mail ballot is a useful tool if the group has a membership that is spread out, such as a group in a rural area or a group composed of members who may live in another part of the country for part of the year; "snowbird" homeowner's association members residing in Florida condos only in the winter, for instance, need mail ballots sent up north other months of the year.

A warning is in order when the nominating ballot

and the mail ballot are used: Members may not be aware that others are not eligible for some reason, or do not wish to serve. Some groups insert a list of those not eligible to be nominated in the nominating ballots; in mail ballots, a request can be made to members who do not wish to serve to notify the secretary of their position on serving. Additionally, nominations are not secret the way they would be if made on a written ballot at a meeting.

 FACT

> Some groups require nominations by petition. This method ensures that a candidate is supported by members, not just someone eager to be part of an election for publicity or ego's sake. This petition can be mailed to members for them to sign to show their support.

Conducting Elections

Nominations have been made. Phone lines have been buzzing as members discuss candidates and urge each other to show up and vote. Finally, election time is here!

The voting process is a time-honored democratic tradition. It's important to the health and well-being of every group or organization to conduct elections with integrity and not rush the process. If there are opposing factions and controversial candidates, both sides should be invited to participate on the tellers' committee to make sure the election is not contested.

Follow the Bylaws

Do your organization's bylaws contain instructions on how the vote will be taken? Is it to be by voice? Ballot? Roll call?

Voice votes give a sense of immediacy. Members know fairly quickly who has won. However, voice votes don't allow for write-in candidates as a ballot does. Roll calls prevent confusion; maybe that loud member makes it sound like there are more votes for her candidate than others.

If there is nothing in the bylaws about voting, a member can make an incidental motion that specifies the methods of voting. This motion must be seconded, is not debatable, is amendable, and needs a majority vote.

Time for the Vote

The vote is about to be taken. Quick! Make sure there is a quorum! Remember, nothing can happen if there is no quorum. The election would be declared null and void if contested.

 QUESTION?

Is there no quorum?
Remember that a member can call for a recess. Members can then call others and see if they can attend the meeting right away. See Chapter 8 for information on how to do this.

Voice Votes

If your group is using a voice vote, the chair takes the vote by saying, "All those in favor of [John Smith] for president, say 'aye.'" Then she says, "All those opposed, say 'no.'" After the vote for each candidate, the chair announces the result, then proceeds to the next officer to be elected.

If one candidate immediately receives a majority vote, then the voting for that office can stop right there. Some parliamentarians feel that the first candidate voted on often gets the majority of the votes. This is why many suggest written ballots. Seeing all the candidates in print may cause members who vote to consider the other candidates for that office more seriously.

Was there a tie or did no one receive a majority vote? Then voting has to continue until a candidate is elected. Sometimes this can take a while. Your group or organization bylaws should be consulted regarding voting procedure here; some have found they need a special procedure to follow. If there isn't one established, a voice vote should be taken again for those offices for which there was a tie or a lack of a majority vote. Voting must continue until there is a majority vote for one candidate.

Ballot Votes

Ballot elections are addressed two different ways: One ballot can contain all of the candidates running for office, or different ballots can be used for each office once the membership has finished with nominations. If your group is large, preparing a printed ballot with all offices is a good idea. Most groups that meet in annual conventions and vote at that time definitely find it's best to use a printed ballot. Just as with voice votes, if there is a tie or a lack of majority vote, ballot elections must continue until a candidate is elected. Again, consult your bylaws for any special rules specific to your group or organization that may have been made. If there are none, then Robert's Rules state that a new ballot should be drawn up with those offices that need another election and the names of those who were listed for those offices (slips of paper are fine here). Then members vote again.

 ESSENTIAL

> It's best to conduct elections at the beginning of a meeting. If there should be a problem with a tie vote or a lack of majority, voting may take a while. You don't want to risk losing a quorum if members have to leave.

Hopefully, this will produce a majority vote for a candidate. If it doesn't, the voting must take place again—and again—until a majority has been attained. If a mail ballot was used, another mailing of a new ballot must be done. Since this can become a tedious process, groups or organizations are advised to be specific about how to deal with this possibility before it becomes a reality. A new ballot should be made with those offices and the names of candidates for them. Voting continues until a majority vote elects a candidate.

Individual Ballots

Smaller groups and organizations sometimes use individual ballots. These are handed out by the tellers after nominations are closed. Members write down the name of the candidate they want elected to an office.

Tellers then collect the ballots, tabulate them, and report on the results to the chair, who announces the name of the member who has been elected. This step must be repeated with each office. If there are a number of directors who are being voted on at one time, the members receiving a majority are elected.

Roll Call Voting

Roll call voting isn't recommended for large groups, as it would take too much time. But for small groups, it can be a quick and easy voting procedure. The secretary calls out the member's name, and he or she can either vote for one candidate for an office, one at a time, *or* vote for the entire list of candidates for office. The secretary should record the vote and, for accuracy's sake, restate it. The downside of voting this way is that the voting is public, not private. Members should carefully consider this when deciding on the method of voting.

Mail Vote

Just as nominations can be taken by mail, and e-mail, so, too, can votes. This is a real timesaver for a large group or one that covers a large area.

This is a time when a plurality vote is a good idea. If a candidate doesn't receive a majority vote, then the candidate who receives the most votes wins; this will eliminate any need for a new election. However, voting is not private in this method, since the secretary will know who sent which ballot.

Election Motions

There are several motions regarding elections that should be helpful to your group or organization. No one wants to see an entire meeting taken up with elections if it can be helped. If the vote is being taken by ballot and it seems as though everyone has voted, a member can make a motion to close the polls. Because this is a motion that limits the rights of members, it will require a second and a two-thirds vote to adopt. Of course, this motion should not be entertained by the chair if any members are still voting.

What if, for some reason, members arrive a little late and the polls are closed, but they want to vote? Perhaps there is a legitimate reason—maybe they were caught in bad weather or a traffic jam. A member may make a motion to open the polls. This will take just a majority vote to put it into effect (because it doesn't take away members' rights, it gives them rights).

Finalizing the Election

The votes are in, they're counted, and it's official—officers have been elected. The tellers' committee gives its report to the chair and reads the report to the membership. Then the chair should announce the list of new officers by saying, "The members have elected: [names and the offices to which they have been elected]."

The chair should ask these newly elected officers if they accept their positions. Hopefully, they all will accept; if not, a new election must take place immediately unless there is some provision in the bylaws that states a different procedure. Those members who are elected take office immediately—again, unless the bylaws say otherwise. Some groups hold installation ceremonies but whether such a ceremony is held or not does not prevent officers from immediately serving.

Keeping It Legal—Things to Remember

Remember that a quorum needs to be present throughout the election. Be very careful about this so that the election isn't contested. If a quorum is not present, the meeting needs to be adjourned and the election continued at another date.

Tellers should cast their votes with the membership before they assume their duties in collecting and tabulating the votes. If there is any question about the way a ballot is marked, they should take the matter to the chair to ask the membership what they wish to do.

Did a member get nominated for an office and elected to two offices? She gets to choose in which office to serve, and there must be another vote on a candidate for the open office.

QUESTION?

What if there is only one candidate for an office?
That's acceptable. If there was just one candidate nominated for an office and your group bylaws don't mandate a ballot vote, the chair can declare the candidate elected by general consent.

The rules about nominations and elections aren't complicated, but they do require careful attention to detail. No group or organization can function for long if it doesn't uphold the democratic ideals of fair and impartial elections. Good officers with integrity and the desire to help further the goals of the group are necessary to its health and longevity. Will you nominate a candidate for office? Will you be nominated? If you're interested in serving, by all means, let someone know. And go for it!

Robert's Rules have served as the authority on parliamentary procedure for groups and organizations for more than a hundred years. While some aspects of them have changed, Robert's Rules, like the U.S. Constitution, have stood the test of time. If it's a democratic group or organization, it probably uses the rules as the standard for parliamentary procedure.

The use of technology continues to alter the way that meetings are conducted. Perhaps it's not too far-fetched to think that one day there will be holo-meetings. Science fiction? Perhaps. But groups and organizations need to make certain that the use of technology related to meetings embraces the true touchstone of Robert's Rules—that it creates a deliberative assembly, one where all members may be seen and heard and may engage in democratic debate over important matters. Guarding that precious right to deliberative assembly is the responsibility of members and officers alike.

The Everything® Robert's Rules Book has been written to help you learn more about a way to participate in your group or organization. It's hoped that you will enjoy participating in your group or organization more with the information you've learned from this book. Here's wishing you success, whether you decide to continue as a member or serve as an officer!

Appendix A
Glossary of Terms

abstain:
Refrain from voting.

ad hoc:
Formed for a temporary need (e.g., ad hoc committee).

adjourn:
End a meeting.

adjourned meeting:
A continuation of a meeting that was adjourned until a future time but is being held before the next regular session.

adopt:
To accept a motion and put it into effect.

agenda:
Specific list of items that will be considered/acted upon at a meeting. Also called **order of business**.

amend:
Change or modify a motion.

amendment:
Proposed alteration or change to a motion.

annual meeting:
Yearly meeting of stockholders or members of a group or organization. Includes election of officers and directors.

appeal:
Question or disagree with the chair's decision.

assembly:
Group of people who have organized and gathered together to conduct business.

audio conference:
Telephone conference.

aye:
A "yes" vote is sometimes referred to in discussion as an "aye" vote.

ballot:
Piece of paper used to cast a vote.

board:

Body of officials with advisory or managerial authority that sets policy for an organization. It's considered to be a form of an assembly.

business:

Matters or items brought before the meeting for action.

bylaws:

The "master document" of rules for governing a group or organization.

call for the orders of the day:

A motion to alert the chair that an item of business is to be brought up at a specific meeting at a specific time.

call to order:

The chair's opening to a meeting. Also, the chair's instruction to a member who is disruptive in some way.

chair:

The presiding officer of the group or organization, usually the president but it may be any officer the president so designates.

committee:

Group of members who are elected or appointed by organization to study or handle a task. A committee is not an assembly like a board.

committee of the whole:
The entire group functions as a committee to consider a matter.

constitution:
Document that states the basic principles and rules of a group or organization.

convene:
Direction to the group to assemble (come to order to start a meeting).

convention:
Meeting of members assembled for a common, specific purpose.

credentials committee:
Group of members who are elected or appointed who verify a member's ability to vote.

debate:
Discussion of a motion prior to a vote.

delegate:
Member who represents other members at a meeting (usually a conference or convention).

dilatory:
Statement, motion, or action that's designed to obstruct or delay a meeting.

division of the assembly:
Retaking a vote by voice or show of hands when the count has been questioned.

division of a motion:
Breaking up a complex motion into separate, independent motions to make it easier for members to understand and vote upon. Also known as division of a question.

executive committee or board:
Committee composed of officers of a group, often including the immediate past president.

executive session:
A meeting or a part of a meeting in which the proceedings are kept secret.

ex officio:
Membership on a board or committee by virtue of holding an official position in a group. (For example, the vice president of the United States serves ex officio as president of the U.S. Senate.)

extend debate:
To officially increase the time members may debate an issue.

floor:
The right of a member to speak, to address a meeting

and have the attention of the membership, as in "obtaining the floor."

gavel:
A small hammer that chairs sometimes rap once or twice to open or close a meeting.

incidental motion:
A motion that arises from another motion.

in order:
Parliamentary term for "correct."

lay on the table:
Set aside temporarily.

limit debate:
To officially restrict the amount of time members may debate an issue.

main motion:
Any motion that introduces business at a meeting.

majority:
More than half of the members who are present and voting on an issue. Members who don't vote aren't counted when determining majority.

meeting:
Gathering or assembly of members to conduct business.

minutes:
Official record of what transpired at a meeting as recorded by the group secretary.

motion:
Proposal for action by a group at a meeting. Also called a question.

move:
To make a motion.

notice of meeting:
Official announcement of a meeting and its particulars (date, time, place, purpose).

order of business:
Agenda. The order in which items on the agenda will be taken up by the membership.

orders of the day:
Business that is to be taken up at a particular time and day. Members can make a privileged motion to insist that this be done.

out of order:
Statement or action that the chair declares is not appropriate or correct parliamentary practice.

parliamentarian:
Someone who is expert in parliamentary procedure.

parliamentary authority:
The rules of order that a group uses as its final (binding) authority on parliamentary procedure.

parliamentary inquiry:
Member's question to the chair about correctness of parliamentary procedure.

pending motion:
Any motion that is on the floor.

plurality:
In matters of voting, the greatest number of votes given to one candidate in a field of three or more choices (this may or may not be a majority of the votes).

point of information:
Question to the chair asking for more information (but not on parliamentary procedure).

point of order:
A question or statement by a member about a potential violation of the rules, which must be raised at the time it occurs.

point of privilege:
Request for immediate attention to a matter that affects members, such as safety or comfort.

postpone indefinitely:

To put off a motion for an indefinite period. This motion then can't be considered at the meeting in progress.

postpone to definite time:

Put off consideration of a motion to a specific future date.

presiding officer:

Also known as the chair. Usually the president but can also be an officer the president designates to preside over (run) the meeting.

previous question:

Motion to close debate on a main motion and put it to a vote immediately.

privileged motion:

Motion that addresses a matter of importance that affects the comfort and safety of a member. It can interrupt any business on the floor.

program:

Agenda for a meeting, which may include a speaker, meal, and/or social function.

pro tem:

Temporary.

proxy:
Power to act on behalf of someone else, usually used in absentee voting (not recommended for regular meetings).

question:
See **previous question**.

quorum:
The official number of members required to conduct business. This number is established by the group's or organization's bylaws.

rank of motion:
One motion has more importance than another. For example, privileged motions always assume precedence over other motions because privileged motions concern conditions such as the comfort or safety of members (the meeting room is too warm, and so on).

recess:
A short break in a meeting.

reconsider:
A motion to review a previous decision and take another vote.

refer to committee:
Send a matter to a committee for study and recommendation of action.

regular meeting:

A scheduled meeting of a group or organization.

rescind:

To nullify a vote on a matter at a previous meeting. A two-thirds majority is required.

roll call vote:

Voice vote where members respond by saying "yes" or "no" when their names are called.

second:

To confirm that another member wants a motion considered (debated). A member states, "I second the motion" or "Second."

session:

One or more meetings on one issue; each meeting continues the work of the previous meeting in a session.

special meeting:

Meeting called to discuss one or more specific topics; no other topics may be discussed at this meeting.

subsidiary motion:

A motion that disposes of another motion. Also called a secondary motion.

take from the table:
Motion to bring back a motion that was previously before the membership.

tellers:
Members appointed or elected to help with elections who distribute ballots, collect and count them, then report the results to the chair.

time and place at which to adjourn:
Motion that sets up a time and place for the next meeting, usually done by temporary groups or organizations that may not have an established meeting place. This motion is not used to adjourn a meeting.

treasurer's report:
The financial report of the group or organization.

two-thirds vote:
A vote that has twice as many members voting for as those against.

unanimous consent:
Also called general consent. When no members object to a motion, there is unanimous or general consent, and there does not need to be a vote on a matter.

unfinished business:
Any matters carried over from a previous meeting. Also

includes any motions that have been postponed to the current meeting.

videoconference:

Meeting where participants are connected through the use of television (there is a picture as well as sound).

withdraw a motion:

A member takes back a motion he or she made. This can be done until it's stated by the chair. After that, the membership must give permission to withdraw.

Appendix B

Guide to Common Motions

These motions are the most frequently used or most important motions to know. Keep this list handy for quick reference.

Main Motion

This is a motion that you make to present new business before your group or organization. To make this motion, a member rises, addresses the chair, and says, "I move to [insert the content of the motion here]." Or, the member can say, "I move that [insert the content of the motion here]." This motion can also be in the form of a resolution: "Resolved, that the Goodwill Community Club supports the passage of the City Parks Proposal and recommends that the city council vote in favor of it at their next meeting."

Postpone Indefinitely

Want to get rid of the main motion for the length of the meeting without having the membership debate it and vote on it? Then postpone indefinitely is your motion. A member should say, "I move to postpone the motion indefinitely."

Postpone indefinitely needs a second, can't be amended (however, it can be amended while motion is pending), and can be debated (and debate is allowed on the main motion's merits). Reconsideration allowed if an affirmative vote is received.

Amend

This is a motion you make to amend (change) the motion that has just been proposed. Perhaps the motion isn't clear enough or is too complicated. The member who proposed the motion doesn't own it, so anyone is free to amend it. If the motion is long, suggest separating it into two or more motions. Substitute words, or insert or delete those that are complicating the motion. Write the changes to the motion if necessary so that it will be easy to see that the motion will be better. A caution: don't try to amend a motion you're not in favor of—that's making a dilatory tactic, one that is trying to waste the time of the membership or just be a nuisance, period.

Amend must have a second and is debatable (only to the amendment, not to the content of the original motion). Majority or two-thirds vote, depending on the motion itself.

Refer to a Committee

Sometimes a motion needs further study. An excellent motion to make is the motion to refer to committee.

Refer needs a second and is debatable (debate must be on referring to committee, not on the content of the original motion).

Postpone to a Certain Time

Perhaps your group or organization has already had a long meeting when a member rises and wants to make a motion. Or the motion itself is controversial and you sense that this would not be a good time to be discussing it. Not that it's a matter that needs to be referred to a committee, it's just that the next meeting would be better—members might be more receptive, or those who would speak for or against the motion could be on hand. This is the time to make a motion to postpone to a certain time. Decide the time this motion should be postponed to before you rise to make the motion.

Postpone to a certain time needs a second and is debatable.

Limit or Extend Limits of Debate

Does it seem that everyone wants to speak for or against a motion? Or that the ten minutes per member that's stated in the bylaws just isn't a good idea for this particular debate—you need more or less time? Then limit or extend limits of debate is the motion for you.

Limit or extend limits of debate requires a second and a two-thirds vote because it takes away the rights of members.

Previous Question

Perhaps there has been enough debate on a main motion. There have been amendments . . . even amendments to amendments! And enough debate! It might be time to move the previous question. This motion stops debate and sends the motion to a vote. The member should say, "I move the previous question" or "I move to close debate and take the vote."

Previous question requires a second and a two-thirds vote because it takes away the rights of members.

No discussion

Lay on the Table

Something has come up—perhaps it is time for a scheduled program or there are items that are really more important to take care of at a particular meeting. The motion that was being discussed needs to stand aside, so to speak. This is the time to make a motion to lay on the table. A caution: this motion can't be used to get rid of a motion or postpone it. Also, there is no such motion as "table a motion." Lay on the table may be what people mean when they use this term.

Lay on the table needs a second, is not amendable, and is not debatable.

Call for the Orders of the Day

Is there a specific time that a matter must be taken up? Perhaps it's the night for elections. If there is an order of the day, a member should rise and call for the orders of the day. That way, something important is not left to wait and wait and wait and perhaps not be taken care of before members start to drift out the door because it's late and the meeting gets adjourned.

Call for the orders of the day needs a second and is debatable.

Raise a Question of Privilege

Is there something that is making members uncomfortable, such as a very warm or very cold room? Is the sound turned off on the microphone and members in the back of the room can't hear? Has an unsafe condition just been noticed? It's time for a question of privilege, which takes precedence over all motions. A member should say, "I rise to a question of privilege concerning the assembly." The chair will ask what the question is, and the member should say, "It's too cold," or whatever the situation is, and then sit down. The chair will rule on the question.

Recess, Adjourn, and Fix the Time to Which to Adjourn

Recess: Is the meeting going into overtime? Perhaps the meeting is running late, or it's getting close to mealtime. Members want to keep the meeting going and not adjourn, but they need a short break. Or, members have shown up for a meeting but there's no quorum, so they want to hit the phones and call others to come to the meeting. A member can make a motion for a recess by saying, "I move to take a recess for [specify the amount of time]."

Recess needs a second, is amendable only for the length of time, and is not debatable. It can't be reconsidered if the majority vote is no, but it can be made again a little later in the meeting.

Adjourn: The time has come to close the meeting. Members don't have to wait for the chair to decide this—they can do so. A member should say, "I move to adjourn."

Adjourn needs a second and is not amendable or debatable.

Fix the time to which to adjourn: This is a motion to continue the current meeting to a later time; it doesn't adjourn the current meeting. A member should say, "I move that when this meeting adjourns, it adjourns to meet [say when]." Fix the time to which to adjourn needs a second, can be amended only as to time and date, and is not debatable.

Motions That Can Be Debated

- Main motion
- Postpone indefinitely
- Amend
- Refer to a committee
- Postpone to a certain time
- Appeal from the decision of the chair
- Rescind
- Amend something previously adopted
- Reconsider
- Recess (when it's an incidental main motion)
- Fix the time to which to adjourn (when it's an incidental main motion)

Motions That Can't Be Debated

- Dispense with the reading of the minutes
- Withdraw a motion
- Suspend the rules
- Limit or extend the limits of debate
- Previous question (close debate, proceed to vote)
- Call for orders of the day
- Raise a question of privilege
- Recess
- Adjourn/Fix the time to which to adjourn
- Point of order

- Object to consideration of a motion
- Division of the assembly/Division of the question
- Incidental motions that relate to voting when subject is pending

Motions Requiring Majority Vote

- Fix the time to which to adjourn
- Adjourn
- Recess
- Lay on the table
- Postpone to a certain time
- Refer to a committee
- Amend
- Postpone indefinitely
- Main motion
- Request permission to withdraw a question
- Take from the table
- Reconsider
- Rescind (needs previous notice)
- Amend something adopted (needs previous notice)
- Reopen nominations/polls

If previous notice is given, the following need only a majority vote:

- Rescind
- Discharge a committee
- Amend something previously adopted

Motions Requiring Two-Thirds Vote

Any motion that takes away rights from members will require a two-thirds vote. Examples of these rights are the right to conduct business by the known and established rules of the group or organization; the right to be informed of pending action, to debate, and to vote. Motions that always require a two-thirds vote:

- Previous question (close debate)
- Limit or extend debate
- Close nominations or polls
- Suspend the rules
- Object to the consideration of a question
- Make a special order

If previous notice has not been given, the following need a two-thirds vote:

- Rescind
- Discharge a committee
- Amend something previously adopted

Appendix C
Additional Resources

Helpful Web sites for information on Robert's Rules:

www.robertsrules.com
The official home page of *Robert's Rules of Order Newly Revised.* Includes a question-and-answer forum.

www.parliamentarians.org
Professional site of the National Association of Parliamentarians. Offers news, membership, independent study course.

www.parliamentaryprocedure.org
Professional site of the American Institute of Parliamentarians. Parliamentary materials, correspondence courses, newsletters.

www.constitution.org
The 1915 edition of *Robert's Rules,* maintained by the Constitution Society. Lesson outlines provided for further study.

www.robertsrules.org
A quick reference for running meetings effectively, with summary of rules. For middle/high school students.

www.roberts-rules.com
Practical tips on parliamentary procedure, updated monthly by the California State Association of Parliamentarians. A how-to site, with examples; in layman's language for the beginner.

www.rulesonline.com
Full 1915 edition of Robert's Rules, with an index and a keyword search. Easy-to-use site for submitting a question, taking a parliamentary quiz, or linking to over fifty parliamentary Web sites.

www.parlipro.org
The companion to RulesOnline.com. Educational and fun Web site with brain teasers, FAQs, keyword search, Web links. Very helpful for the high school student studying parliamentary procedure.

www.okparliamentarians.org
Promotes the study and use of Robert's Rules of Order in Oklahoma at the state level, with links to applying them at the local units.

www.nelsonpena.8m.com
The *Robert's Rules of Order* text in Spanish, maintained by a professor at the University of Puerto Rico.

Index

We Have
EVERYTHING®
For Business!

Everything® Business Planning Book
ISBN: 1-58062-491-X
$12.95 ($17.95 CAN)

Everything® Coaching and
Mentoring Book
ISBN: 1-58062-730-7
$14.95 ($19.95 CAN)

Everything® Fundraising Book
ISBN: 1-58062-953-9
$14.95 ($19.95 CAN)

Everything® Home-Based
Business Book, 2nd edition
ISBN: 1-59337-266-2
$14.95 ($19.95 CAN)

Everything® Landlording Book
ISBN: 1-59337-143-8
$14.95 ($19.95 CAN)

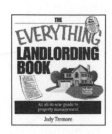

Everything® Leadership Book
ISBN: 1-58062-513-4
$12.95 ($17.95 CAN)

Everything® Managing People
Book, 2nd edition
ISBN: 1-59869-143-0
$14.95 ($19.95 CAN)

Everything® Negotiating Book
ISBN: 1-59337-152-7
$14.95 ($19.95 CAN)

Everything® and everything.com® are registered trademarks of F+W Publications, Inc.

Everything® Online Business Book
ISBN: 1-58062-320-4
$12.95 ($17.95 CAN)

Everything® Project
Management Book
ISBN: 1-58062-583-5
$12.95 ($17.95 CAN)

Everything® Selling Book
ISBN: 1-58062-319-0
$14.95 ($19.95 CAN)

Everything® Start Your Own
Business Book, 2nd edition
ISBN: 1-59337-661-8
$14.95 ($19.95 CAN)

Available wherever books are sold!
To order, call 800-258-0929, or visit us at *everything.com*